"WHEN WE PAY OUR FIVE BUCKS AND SEAT OURSELVES AT TENTH-ROW CENTER IN A THEATRE SHOWING A HORROR MOVIE, WE ARE DARING THE NIGHTMARE."

—Stephen King

Now enjoy the best seat in the house to view the inside story of such King-sized horror hits as:

☐ CARRIE, directed by the audacious Brian De Palma (remember that last shot of Sissy Spacek's hand?).

☐ CREEPSHOW, with a screenplay by King himself, plus his debut as a screen actor.

☐ CUJO, which King calls "one of the scariest things you'll ever see. It's terrifying."

☐ THE DEAD ZONE, perhaps the greatest of all King films.

☐ CHRISTINE, the ultimate drive-in movie.

☐ STAND BY ME, the "sleeper" smash that proved King's vision went beyond horror to humanity.

☐ And all the other triumphs that have made America's bestselling writer King of the Screen as well!

Previous books on Stephen King that TIM UNDERWOOD and CHUCK MILLER have edited are FEAR ITSELF: *The Horror Fiction of Stephen King* and KINGDOM OF FEAR: *The World of Stephen King*, both available in Plume editions. JEFF CONNER is a scriptwriter, publisher of Scream Press, and a film producer specializing in the horror genre.

STEPHEN KING GOES TO HOLLYWOOD

A LAVISHLY ILLUSTRATED GUIDE TO ALL THE FILMS BASED ON STEPHEN KING'S FICTION

PRODUCED BY
TIM UNDERWOOD
AND
CHUCK MILLER
WRITTEN BY
JEFF CONNER

A PLUME BOOK

NEW AMERICAN LIBRARY

NEW YORK AND SCARBOROUGH, ONTARIO

Stephen King Goes to Hollywood is also available in an NAL Books hardcover edition published by New American Library and, simultaneously in Canada, by The New American Library of Canada Limited.

 PLUME TRADEMARK REG. U.S. PAT. OFF. AND FOREIGN COUNTRIES
REG. TRADEMARK—MARCA REGISTRADA
HECHO EN HARRISONBURG, VA., U.S.A.

SIGNET, SIGNET CLASSIC, MENTOR, ONYX, PLUME, MERIDIAN AND NAL BOOKS ARE PUBLISHED *in the United States* by NAL PENGUIN INC., 1633 Broadway, New York, New York 10019, *in Canada* by The New American Library of Canada Limited, 81 Mack Avenue, Scarborough, Ontario M1L 1M8

Library of Congress Cataloging-in-Publication Data

Conner, Jeff.
  Stephen King goes to Hollywood.

    1. King, Stephen, 1947–   —Film adaptations.   2. Horror films—United States—History and criticism.   I. Title.
PS3561.I483Z6287   1987   791.43′09′0916   87-11310
ISBN 0-453-00552-7
ISBN 0-452-25937-1

First Printing, August, 1987

1 2 3 4 5 6 7 8 9

PRINTED IN THE UNITED STATES OF AMERICA

CONTENTS

INTRODUCTION: *Interview with Stephen King*. vii

FOREWORD. x

CARRIE. 1

'SALEM'S LOT. 15

THE SHINING. 25

CREEPSHOW. 35

CUJO. 47

THE DEAD ZONE. 55

CHRISTINE. 69

CHILDREN OF THE CORN. 79

FIRESTARTER. 87

CAT'S EYE. 97

SILVER BULLET. 107

MAXIMUM OVERDRIVE. 115

STAND BY ME. 123

STEPHEN KING ON VIDEO. 133

COMING ATTRACTIONS. 141

PHOTO ACKNOWLEDGMENTS

INTERVIEW WITH STEPHEN KING

Stephen King, horror's Maine man, stretches his director's legs at the helm of Maximum Overdrive.

Q: Can you talk about *Maximum Overdrive*—what was it like directing your first movie?

Stephen King: The movie is about all these vehicles going crazy and running by themselves, so we started shooting a lot of gas pedals, clutches, transmissions, things like that, operating themselves. We had one sequence: The gas pedal to the floor, the gas pedal goes up, the clutch goes in, the gear shifts by itself, the clutch comes out, and the gas pedal goes back to the floor again. We were able to shoot everything but the transmission from the driver's-side door. The transmission was a problem, because we kept seeing either a corner of the studio or a reflection.

So I said: This is no problem, we will simply take the camera around to the other side and shoot the transmission from there.

Total silence. Everybody was looking at everybody else. You know what's happening here, right? I'd crossed the axis. It was like farting at the dinner party: Nobody wanted to say you've made a terrible mistake. I didn't get this job because I could direct or because I had any background in film; I got it because I was Stephen King.

So finally [cameraman] Armando Nannuzzi told me I'd crossed the 180-degree axis and that this simply wasn't done, and although I didn't understand what it was, I grasped the idea that it was breaking a rule.

Later on I called George [Romero] up on the phone and I said, "What is this axis shit?" and he laughed his head off, and explained it, and I said, "Can you break it—the rule?" He said, "It's better not to, but if you have to, you can. If you look at *The Battleship Potemkin*" (which I never have), "it crosses the axis all the time, and the guy [Sergei Eisenstein] gets away with it." Then I saw David Lynch and asked him: "What's this about crossing the axis?" and he burst out laughing and said, "That always gets me." And I asked if you could do it, and he gave me this startled look and said, "Stephen, you can do anything. You're the director." Then he paused and said, "But it doesn't cut together."

Q: What effect were you aiming for in *Maximum Overdrive*?

King: I wanted it to move fast. It's a wonderful moron picture, in that sense. It's a really illiterate picture in a lot of ways. There isn't a lot of dialogue in it. It's fast. A lot of things explode. It's very profane, very vulgar, quite violent in some places. We're going to have trouble with the Ratings Board, I guess.

Q: Did you pay attention to character relations in the story or did you want to wow the audience with spectacle?

King: I'm interested in my people. One of the few really sensible things that anybody said at the story conference that we had at MGM in L.A.—those people, what an alien mentality!—But somebody did say that if the characters don't stand out and this is just a movie about machines, it'll be a bad picture. Their solution was to suggest that a lot of dialogue and scenes between the major characters be added for character and texture. I was always calling them the jumbo "John! Oh, Martha!" scenes, because they're like soap operas. We shot 'em. We just cut 'em all out in the editing room, every single one.

It's like that classic moment in *The Swarm* where Fred MacMurray and Olivia De Havilland have this scene, and Fred says the equivalent—I swear this is true—he doesn't exactly say this, he says something like, "The bees are coming, and we'll all probably be killed, but thank Christ I'm not impotent anymore." That's really what they want.

I'm interested in character eccentricity, in the interactions of daily life that you don't necessarily see on the screen. I'm not particularly interested in character in the traditional sense of, let's say, Scorsese. I prefer Hitchcock, because the characters that you find really interesting in his pictures are always in supporting roles, like the old lady who lectures about the birds in *The Birds*: "They can't. It's simply not possible. Their brain pans are too small."

Q: What do you feel are some of the scariest moments in your film adaptations?

King: You mean that scared me in the theater? When that hand comes out of the grave in *Carrie* at the end. Man, I thought I was going to shit in my pants.

Q: You had no idea . . . ?

King: Yeah, I knew they were going to do it, and I still almost shit in my pants. The first time I saw *Carrie* with an audience they previewed it about a week and a half before Halloween. They didn't do a screening in Maine, but they did one in Boston, so my wife and I went down to the theater, and I just looked around in total dismay, because the regular picture that they were showing was *Norman, Is That You?* with Redd Foxx. The theater was entirely full of black people. We looked like two little grains of salt in a pepper shaker, and we thought: This audience is just going to rate the hell out of this picture. What are they going to think about a skinny little white girl with her menstrual problems? And that's the way it started, and then, little by little, they got on her side, you know, and when she started doing her shtick, I mean, they're going, "Tear it up!" "Go for it!" and all this other stuff. These two guys were talking behind us, and we were listening to them, and at the end they're putting on their coats and getting ready to leave. Suddenly this hand comes up, and these two big guys screamed along with everyone else, and one of them goes, "That's it! That's it! She ain't never gonna be right!" And I knew it was going to be a hit. □

FOREWORD

Rob Reiner and crew set up a scene with a stunt corpse and the four young stars of Stand By Me.

Hollywood and horror have been going steady since the Edison Studios' 10-minute production of *Frankenstein* in 1907. Yet this adaptation was just one entrant in a vast array of one-reel photoplays being issued at the time. In their competitive search for viable plots and stories, the young film companies quickly turned to the classics for inspiration.

The reasoning behind appropriating the "classics" was elementary: they had time-tested plots, high visibility and low story costs. The early film promoters soon discovered that the moving pictures' initial appeal as a technological novelty was in itself not sufficiently profitable. As theatrical exhibition blossomed, the competition for customers became quite fierce. Some theatres changed their shows as often as three times a week. By necessity, the larger theatre owners and film distributors (or "exchanges") entered the production side of the motion picture business as an effective means of ensuring a steady flow of new titles for their screens. If they couldn't buy or become partners with a filmmaking company, they simply started their own. (An ugly patents war was raging at the time as Edison tried to retain economic control of domestic motion picture technology.)

The new "studios," the factories where the exhibitor's product was made, were owned and controlled by these distribution and exhibition syndicates. The film industry quickly became vertically integrated. The major companies were active in all areas of the motion picture business cycle: production, distribution and exhibition. Film production moved to California, first to San Francisco, then Hollywood, and the studios, with their excitement and star personalities, became erroneously fixed in the public's mind as running the whole show. The Hollywood film moguls were only responsible for manufacturing the "shows," being partnered (or in their minds, "shackled") with the distribution companies in New York, who took care of the "business."

It was a great business, too—even during the Depression—up until peace broke out after WWII. Sixty million Americans regularly made the movies a part of their entertainment diet (compared with only 20 million today). Significantly, the traditional "peak" periods of film attendance at that time were exactly opposite what they are now. In those days film attendance dropped dramatically during the Christmas and Summer seasons, for the holidays interfered with the citizenry's twice weekly trips to "the show."

Also, the filmgoing public was then truly homogeneous. After 1932, a succession of film review boards did their best to ensure that all films were suitable for all people, no matter the subject matter. At that time, the general public used to *read* regularly for pleasure. Books and literature were very much a topic of discussion, and not just during high school English classes. Every popular book, play or important classic was sure to enjoy some kind of cinematic incarnation, often two or three. After all, with the major six studios each releasing a brand new production every week (not counting serials, newsreels and "B" pictures), it just made good sense to adapt properties already familiar to the audience—an already popular story gave a film an edge on the competition.

From the beginning, the industry recognized that filmmaking was the "research and development" phase in the show business cycle. Their annual slate of new productions was funded entirely by the exhibition and distribution corners of the triangle. But the theatres were forcibly separated from the distribution and production functions through anti-monopolistic government action (culminating in the 1947 Consent Decrees, which are due to expire in the next few years). As a result, the studios, for the first time, were now actually expected to generate income on their own.

Today, Hollywood has changed greatly, and its product has changed as well. The homogeneous audience has fragmented. Now only one person in every five is a regular filmgoer. This year's biggest hit will be seen by no more than 20% of the American public. Once, every major book was snatched up by film producers, but now television is the medium of choice for "the big book," the popular biographical story, or the topical melodrama or "problem picture." *Shogun, The Atlanta Child Murders, The Winds of War, Death of a Centerfold, Smiley's People, Fatal Vision, Friendly Fire, An Early Frost, At Mother's Request*; the list of films made-for-television grows by the week.

There is a school of thought that contends that trying to reduce a 400-page novel to a 130-page screenplay while retaining little more than a token degree of faithfulness to plot or character development is essentially an impossible task. The conventions and time restraints of film simply do not lend themselves gracefully to the multilevel complexities of the literary experience. It would be more fruitful, this group avers, to expand shorter works into feature-length projects; little would be lost and much could be gained.

Advent of the miniseries addresses the problem of length. Though the screen size may be smaller, television is indeed the home for the modern epic film. And as for expanding short stories into full scripts? Few short stories have the three-act structure Hollywood believes in. Unless the author is extremely popular and the work extremely commercial, it's simpler just to start from scratch with an original screenplay, the story would have to changed so much anyway.

But one theatrical genre has remained essentially the sole domain of the silver screen: horror. Pure, sure, polyunsaturated terror of the gut wrenching, blood-curdling, nail-biting, eye-crossing variety. It's either too nasty for living room entertainment or too vulnerable to commercial interruptions. Who is the most popular writer of horror fiction in the last decade and why is Stephen King so popular with film producers? Why aren't other consistent fiction bestsellers like V.C. Andrews or John Saul getting their books onto the screen by the bucketful? Basically because you can get a funding deal when you have a Stephen King property under option.

Stephen King's books not only race to the top of the hardcover bestsellers lists and stay there; they've also created an army of ardent fans, fans whose allegiance to King reaches almost religious intensity. He's a veritable ayatollah of terror! What production executive could ignore such marketing potential and industry cachet?

Additionally, King's plot concepts are simple and easy to digest, often inspired by the classic horror and science fiction films of his youth. ("Sid, IT you'll love. Every monster Universal Pictures ever made is in there.") And, most important, King's stories are essentially character-oriented with lots of conflict. Conflict and characters are what Hollywood movies are all about.

Only a fool or a rich man makes a picture without a distribution deal in place, and the largest funding source for films are the distributors. These days, it's hard to get an original project funded that does not have some easily marketable element (other than the genre itself): either a hot star, a topical subject or setting, or widely-popular underlying source material—in short, an easily exploitable element.

An easily exploitable marketing element helps to ensure that the picture will "open." (Meaning that, when 1300 theatres are playing your films the seats aren't all empty.) If the picture will open, then a funding deal is made and the picture produced. This is why so many "packaged" movies get made, pictures initiated as marketing concepts first, good pictures second (such as *Legal Eagles*). As a bestselling, name-brand author, the name "Stephen King" provides just such a marketing element, over and above the quality of his work.

The financial risk, or "downside," of genre filmmaking is ever decreasing, thanks to the increasing ancillary monies available from the videocassette marketplace. With the videorecorder "universe" expected to achieve a 57% household penetration by the end of 1987, it's not surprising to begin observing many theatrically-released genre features generating far more revenues through sales of videocassettes than box office tickets. Indeed, the phenomenon of "direct-to" video productions (features made exclusively for the home market), have been pioneered by low-low budget horror titles, which often compensate for lack of production values by increasing the content of their graphic violence and gore. Once again, horror breaks new commercial ground.

It *is* unusual for one author to have so many pictures made from his books, even for such a prolific writer as Mr. King. Taken as a whole his work forms a formidable and ever-growing body of fiction, which shows no signs of slowing down. This snowballing blizzard of terror is creating a sub-genre within the horror field: the Stephen King film. Even this category can be subdivided into productions done with or without the writer's involvement. King himself has been bitten by the Hollywood bug, a unique infection that has led not only to his transforming his own works into screenplays, but also to Stephen King—director, as well. (Others in the author-to-director sub-set include such genre writers as Michael Crichton, William Peter Blatty, and, now, Clive Barker).

Whither Stephen King? And his trip to Hollywood? The Horror Well never runs dry and many young filmmakers dip into its waters for sure-sell projects to help their careers. The names of Francis Ford Coppola, Brian De Palma, John Sayles, James Cameron, George Romero, David Cronenberg, Wes Craven, Lewis Teague, John Landis, John Carpenter, Tobe Hooper, and Joe Dante come quickly to mind. Some, like Carpenter, Landis and Dante return to this bloody font from time to time, others choose never to leave (like Cronenberg and the Italian splatter kings, Lucio Fulci and Dario Argento). Some few should never have left (like Hooper, Craven and Romero). Still other directors, already with successful careers, decide to drop by for a taste of grue, either to rejuvenate their palettes (like Paul Schrader) or simply for no apparent reason (like Stanley Kubrick, for Christsakes).

It's been said that the successful horror picture places ordinary people in extraordinary situations (and great comedies do just the reverse). It's also been noted that in genre entertainment, a good gimmick or "catch" will overcome bad writing, and vice versa. King performs both tricks with compulsive ease. So while we may have read books about psychokinetic kids, hissing vampires, possessed places, or diseased animals, they probably haven't had the richness of "ordinary" characterization that King injects into his "extraordinary" storylines.

But the film business is much more fickle than the literary marketplace, which often supports careers as long as a country western singer's (once you're in, you're in). In terms of popularity, the films of Stephen King's books haven't performed nearly so well as the books themselves, but horror films never do extremely well (neither do heavy violence pictures). Sure, *The Godfather, The French Connection*, and *The Exorcist* were all box office record-setters, but their earnings are outshined by more wholesome fare like Spielberg and/or Lucas films and, when adjusted for inflation, *The Sound of Music*, *Gone With the Wind*, and other such "family" pictures.

Still, the horror genre is a market you can count on. Its fans are loyal filmgoers, eager to see practically anything, whether a "calendar" film (*New Year's Evil, Happy Birthday to Me, Mother's Day*), an "ing" or "or" pictures (*The Mutilator, The Burning, Re-Animator, The Howling*), or one of those titles featuring Roman numerals (you know the ones). So it's no revelation that the world's bestselling horror writer, who broke out of the genre ghetto into big time hardcover literature, who has entire books of critical essays devoted to his works, is now also the number one target for enterprising film producers. And what writer can resist that kind of attention?

Let's review these theatrical versions of Stephen King's works. How are they as entertainment vehicles? as faithful representations of King's art and intentions? as films in and of themselves? King is a genre unto himself, a special flavor in that sanguinary ice cream parlor of shock and suspense. Sometimes you get a double-scoop, sometimes even nuts and cherries on top, but whatever the serving, it's almost certain to be familiar. □

Jeff Conner
Hollywood, California
January, 1987

"So about five years ago I went to him and said, 'I took your idea and I wrote a story about these kids who walk down a railroad track to find the body of a boy.' I didn't think anybody would be too interested in going to look at the body of a dog. I took the main character and I took a lot of things that I had felt when I was a kid and put them into that character, Gordon McChance. But John Irving also says, never believe a writer when he seems to be offering you autobiography, because we all lie. We all edit it and we say, well, this is what happened, but that doesn't make a good story so I'll change it. So it's mostly a lie."
—Speaking of *Stand By Me* at Bellerica Library

"CARRIE"

DIRECTED BY BRIAN DE PALMA

*Behind those perfect smiles, unbridled adolescent cruelty as only
Stephen King can deliver.*

CARRIE (1976)

With few exceptions, film concepts in Hollywood can be reduced
to a single descriptive question, a "log line." *Carrie* asks: Can this
girl's telekinetic powers save her? Or, stated more basically: abused
adolescent seeks revenge, flexes telekinetic muscle. Mayhem ensues.

Simplistic? You bet. Commercial? And how!

The story concerns young Carrie White, a lonely high schooler
alternately tormented by boorish classmates and traumatized by her
Hell and Damnation-obsessed mother. A particularly ugly incident
triggered by her first menstrual cycle results in Carrie being the
intended target for a cruelly thematic "revenge" plot devised by a

Mug shots from Carrie's high school yearbook: Amy Irving (left), Betty Buckley (center) and Nancy Allen (right).

CARRIE

A United Artists release, 11/76. 97 minutes (R). Directed by Brian De Palma. Produced by Paul Monash. Screenplay by Lawrence D. Cohen. Associate Producer: Louis A. Stroller. Director of Photography: Mario Tosi. Editor: Paul Hirsh. Original Music: Pino Donaggio. Art Directors: William Kenny & Jack Fisk. Costume Designer: Rosanna Norton. Special Effects: Gregory M. Auer. Stunt Coordinator: Richard Weiker.

Carrie White . . . . .Sissy Spacek
Margaret White . . . . .Piper Laurie
Sue Snell . . . . .Amy Irving
Tommy Ross. . . . . .William Katt
Chris Hargensen . . . . .Nancy Allen
Billy Nolan . . . . .John Travolta
Miss Collins. . . . . .Betty Buckley
Norma Watson . . . . .P.J. Soles
Mrs. Snell. . . . . .Priscilla Pointer
Freddy . . . . .Michael Talbot

Also: Stefen Gierash, Doug Cox, Harry Gold, Noelle North, Cindy Daly, Dierdre Berthrong, Anson Downes, Rory Stevens, Edie McClurg, Cameron De Palma.

gang of girl nasties. Their vicious taunting of the hysterical girl got them in trouble with the sympathetic gym coach, so naturally they blame Carrie for their punishment. Besides psychological trauma, the onset of menstruation also brings about the awakening of Carrie's nascent telekinetic powers, a new kind of flowing inner strength.

One of the girls realizes the error of her ways and tries to do Carrie a good turn, getting her blond Adonis boyfriend to invite Carrie to the prom as his date. But this gesture backfires when the wicked girls' plot succeeds: Carrie is drenched with pig's blood just as she's crowned queen of the prom. But the humiliated Carrie does more than just get hysterical, she gets even, leaving the gym aflame and littered with bodies. Returning home, the tired and bloody Carrie finds only more betrayal and anguish awaiting her; Mom

The prom before the storm: Tommy Ross (William Katt) and Carrie White's (Sissy Spacek) last moments of true happiness.

3

knows that her little girl is now a tool of the Devil. (What a day!) Their rather pointed discussion leaves Mrs. White stapled to the wall with a variety of household kitchen items, the very sharp kind. The strain is too much to bear, Carrie literally brings down the house, permanently ending her intense adolescent adjustment problems.

This picture really delivered the goods. De Palma's unrestrained use of the flashier aspects of film language, such as elaborate crane and dolly shots, extensive slow-motion, rarely utilized split-screen, and even speeded-up action for comic effect, gave the material the right stylish gloss needed to sell the story's outrageous action and maudlin, even campy, plot elements.

CARRIE was purchased by writer/producer Paul Monash, the creator of television's *Judd for the Defense* and the producer responsible for *Butch Cassidy and the Sundance Kid*, *Slaughterhouse Five* and *The Friends of Eddie Coyle*, the latter two derived from fine novels. While searching for a studio production deal Monash was turned down by Paramount, Fox and others before finally "getting in bed" with United Artists. The studio was attracted to the profitable "supernatural" trend spawned by *Rosemary's Baby* (1968) and multiplied by *The Exorcist* (1973), and they were willing to try out CARRIE as long as the price of "getting pregnant" wasn't too high.

According to King, there was some interest in CARRIE when the pre-publication galleys made the rounds, standard operating procedure between the publishing and motion picture industries. "It just wasn't strong in terms of money. So they [Doubleday] decided to hold it back until publication, gambling that the book would be a hardcover bestseller and the interest in the movie rights would go up again." This didn't exactly come to pass; CARRIE did not burn up the charts. Five months later the property finally did sell. "We didn't do wonderfully well but I got a piece of the action, so the money end of it

---

"The Doubleday sub-rights department came up with three people who wanted to buy it ['Carrie'], and I thought [Paul] Monash seemed like the best go. They said to me after they bought, 'Who would you pick to direct if you could get anybody?' I said 'There's this guy named Brian De Palma, who did a film called SISTERS. It was a scary monster.'"
—with Marty Ketchum, Pat Cadigan & Lewis Shiner.

Betrayed at her most vulnerable, Carrie's powers can't save her from Mom's constant backstabbing.

was all right," King recalled about his first brush with Hollywood. Discussing the basis for CARRIE, King has revealed that it is "derived to a considerable extent from a terrible grade-B movie called *The Brain from Planet Arous* (1958)." This would not be the last time a movie from his youth would resurface in his work.

As a cloutless, first-time novelist, King was obliged to let Doubleday purchase all rights to CARRIE. The author remembers that the Doubleday subsidiary rights department told him that three people wanted to make offers on the book. He felt at the time that producer Paul Monash was the best suitor. "They said to me after they bought it, 'Who would you pick to direct if you could get anybody?' I said, 'There's this guy named Brian De Palma, who did a film called *Sisters*. It was a scary monster.' "

Screenwriter Lawrence D. Cohen's adaptation of King's novel gave young director Brian De Palma a tremendous vehicle with which to successfully portray the real-life horrors of high school (surely one of the lowest levels of Hell). By focusing mainly on doomed Carrie White's situation, Cohen wove a coherent screenplay out of the jumpy, fragmented narrative technique King used in his novel. (Cohen would later be less successful when tackling Peter Straub's horror epic, GHOST STORY.)

Originally budgeted at $1.6 million, the picture actually came in at De Palma's predicted $1.8. *Carrie* went on to be one of the top money-makers of the year, grossing around $30 million domestically and eventually returning over $15 million in film rentals.

It should be briefly noted that the relationship between a film's box office gross (the dollar amount of all tickets sold) and its film rentals is similar to that of a product's retail and wholesale prices. As a general rule, the exhibitor keeps approximately 40% of a picture's box office grosses, paying the rest in "rentals" to the distribution company. To pay for overhead, the distributor charges a 30% "distribution fee" on these rentals. Additionally, the distributor deducts "prints and ads" from the film rentals. These direct, individual costs of making up the film's prints (around $1250 each) and running the advertising and promotion campaigns necessary to "open" the picture, today can run to $7 million for a typical studio picture opening nationally in 900 to 1300 theatres.

Thus, of the $15 million in rentals *Carrie* earned, a $4.5 million distribution fee was charged. Allowing for 1971 media prices, approximately another $3.5 million in prints and ads was deducted.

"I really liked it because the novel is the novel of a young man. I think the first draft of 'Carrie' was done when I was 22, and at the time it was very sober-sided. I was maybe too close to the subject [King had taught high school during that time], and De Palma's film is kind of light and frothy and he gets you at the end when you think it's all over . . ."

—Speaking of *Carrie* at Bellerica Library

Shades of Norman Bates and Lizzie Borden: Piper Laurie cuts a fine figure as Carrie's mommie dearest.

The cost of the picture, plus interest, was then taken out. So, *Carrie's* $30 million box office performance was reduced to $5.2 million before any of the proceeds began reaching the film's producer, who shares half the cash with Warner Bros., the distributor who funded the picture that was made at its studio.

So, after charging interest on the production loan, overhead fees on the studio's services and facilities, and taking fees and salaries all along the way, separate from the distribution costs, Warner Bros. made around a million dollars pure profit on its $1.8 million investment. Thus, all foreign receipts, television sales and cassette sales (after appropriate fees and expenses), as well as any ancillary monies from licensed merchandising or other non-exhibition income, all constitute additional profits.

Yes indeedy, the real money in the movie business is not and has never been in the glamorous world of production. The CPA-ruled realm of distribution is where the big money is. Let us not forget that today's major studios were started some seventy-five years ago as manufacturing facilities for and by the often-feuding film distributors, simply to ensure a dependable flow of new product for their distribution pipelines. Thus were born many great films.

    Carrie came at a pivotal time for De Palma. He had followed the critical and commercial success of his 1973 low-budget shocker, *Sisters*, with the ill-considered "musical horror satire," *The Phantom of the Paradise* for producer Ed Pressman in 1974. After this came the obtuse, Hitchcock-derived *Obsession* in early 1976. The director needed a hit of some kind. "*Carrie* was an intense set . . . there was a lot of pressure from the studio. There weren't many laughs," co-star Amy Irving has been quoted regarding her experiences on the film.

    Actually, some good did come of *Phantom*. Sissy Spacek first worked for De Palma at that time, helping production designer Jack Fisk, her future-husband, with set decoration. This connection, as well as her fine work in *Badlands* (1973), led to their both working again for De Palma on *Carrie*. (Now Spacek no longer had to lug paint cans around, just get one dropped on her.) She has since starred in two films directed by her husband Fisk, *Raggedy Man* (1981) and *Violets Are Blue* (1986).

    Carrie was instrumental in launching a number of careers along with Sissy Spacek's (this was her first starring role, after having debuted as another abused female in 1972's *Prime Cut* with Lee

Blood-plastered Carrie prepares to wreak havoc on her tormentors (left). Relaxing in the family kitchen after a hard night at school.

Curfew time is no problem at the prom as Carrie uses her telekinetic powers to wish everyone a safe drive home.

Marvin). Amy Irving, who played Carrie's friend, would return to star in De Palma's 1978 follow-up, *The Fury*, and later marry another filmmaker, an obscure ex-television director (*Columbo*) named Spielberg. Nancy Allen would marry De Palma and star in several of his subsequent pictures, most notably as menaced hookers in both *Dressed To Kill* and *Blow Out*, before their marriage ended. P.J. Soles would later be slaughtered in John Carpenter's *Halloween*, star with the Ramones in *Rock 'n' Roll High School*, and play opposite Bill Murray in *Stripes*. Television teen-throb John Travolta would re-team with Nancy Allen in *Blow Out* after dancing his way into the box office record books with *Saturday Night Fever* and *Grease*. William Katt subsequently became TV's *The Greatest American Hero* and eventually returned to the horror field in Sean S. Cunningham and Steve Miner's *House*. And look quickly, you'll see Michael Talbot (helping his on-screen girlfriend P.J. Soles rig the prom election), he's now playing agent Zwietek on *Miami Vice*.

The picture also revitalized the career of Piper Laurie, who had retired after her Oscar-winning portrayal of Paul Newman's limping girlfriend in *The Hustler* (1961). Fittingly, she received an Oscar nomination for her portrayal of Carrie White's fanatical mother, and has since remained active with both screen and stage projects. Sissy Spacek also received an Academy Award nomination for *Carrie*. All in all, pretty classy for a low-budget horror movie.

Spacek brought to her role of Carrie White an intense, naturalistic veracity that would become a trademark in her subsequent screen work. Without a body double in sight, the daring actress made the opening nude shower scene startlingly real, even shocking for its time. (Menstruation was then far from the clichéd horror film plot device it has since become.) Spacek did all her own stunts as well, and not without incident: singeing her eyebrows in the gymnasium conflagration and then badly scraping her arm on the sharp, graveside rocks in the film's "gripping" coda (a particularly dedicated piece of method acting as only her arm is visible in the scene).

Spacek was originally slated to play the evil Chris Hargensen, and Carrie Fisher was up for the title role of Carrie! It seems that De Palma sat in on George Lucas's casting sessions for *Star Wars*, as both directors were looking to fill leading roles with young unknowns. With palpable on-screen chemistry between male and female characters a requirement, finding just the right combination of personalities was a lengthy trial and error process of interviews and screen tests. It was at one of these sessions that De Palma first saw Amy Irving. She was being paired with William Katt while Carrie Fisher and Mark Hamill were matched up, and for a time it was uncertain just which couple would be chosen for these two wildly differing pictures. But Lucas finally favored the Hamill/Fisher formula, ensuring their places in the Hollywood firmament. De Palma went with Irving and Katt, who both performed very well for him.

King has noted that after Spacek's casting was announced he was given some grief by those alarmed over the fact that, as described his novel, Carrie White was a solid, beefy girl with a pudding face, a description far different from Spacek's physical appearance. "I didn't give a shit *what* she looked like," King has said, "as long as she could look sort of ugly before and then look nice at the prom." The author saw his characters' inner make-up transcending their looks. "I want to know what my characters feel and what makes them move."

Somewhat of a "method" director himself, De Palma often employs unusual techniques to achieve his effects. One of these is to cast real life mother and daughter actresses in corresponding mother and daughter screen roles. He first did this with Jennifer Salt and her mother, Mary Davenport, in *Sisters* and again with Amy Irving and her mother, Priscilla Pointer (*Dallas*), for *Carrie*. Pointer and Irving would also reteam in *Micki and Maude* and *The Competition*.

For the film's concluding dream sequence, De Palma filmed Irving in slow motion and reverse while she walked backwards along the suburban streets. When projected forwards the results evoke a subtle feeling of displacement, though the cars and birds seen impossibly moving in reverse in the background tend to vitiate the effect if you look closely. Another "backwards" trick De Palma used was to film part of this sequence "night for day," a reversal on the cost-saving "day for night" method often employed to create a nighttime effect through filters and printing techniques.

Another sequence involving camera trickery, later excised from the picture, was a flashback scene of Carrie White as a six-year-old. Spacek herself did most of the sequence, though a little girl was used for a shot of her running from the camera. The illusion of youth was accomplished by having the actress wear appropriate children's clothes and filming her through an oversized picket fence. "It was incredible to watch," Amy Irving has reported. "It was hysterical." This telling critique may well account for the absence of the sequence in the finished film.

Jack Fisk was called upon to destroy the White house for the penultimate finale. De Palma wanted the half-scale version Fisk built to be swallowed up by the earth, while being simultaneously bombarded by large rocks. But it proved to be impossible in getting those pesky boulders to realistically hurtle about on cue, so it was decided that the house would burst into flames instead. The effect works well, though in Stephen King's novel pyrokinesis was never a part of Carrie's mental talents. (That angle would just have to wait for another book, and another film.)

King was very pleased with the film version of CARRIE. "In many ways, the film is more stylish than my book," the author told one interviewer. According to King, the book's first draft was finished when he was 22 and teaching high school English. His characters were composites of the personalities he saw in the classroom, and the results were on the grim side. "I was maybe too close to the subject, and De Palma's film is kind of light and frothy and he gets you at the end when you think it's all over. . . ." □

'SALEM'S LOT

DIRECTED BY TOBE HOOPER

David Soul (center) is surrounded by Barlow and his human helper Straker (James Mason.)

'SALEM'S LOT (1979)

'SALEM'S LOT is, by King's own admission, his take on Bram Stoker's classic tale of a certain Transylvanian's visit to England. Still a high school English instructor at the time, King had taught DRACULA for several semesters, becoming increasingly interested in the novel's strength. One night over dinner a friend brought up the question of what might happen if The Count were to appear in modern day society. King's wife, Tabitha (also a novelist), believed

Free dental floss or the kid gets it! Reggie Nalder does his Nosferatu imitation as Barlow in 'Salem's Lot.

'SALEM'S LOT

A Warner Brothers release, 11/79. (TV miniseries 200 minutes, TV-movie 150 minutes, European theatrical & videocassette version 112) (R). Directed by Tobe Hooper. Produced by Richard Kobritz. Screenplay by Paul Monash. Executive Producer: Stirling Silliphant. Director of Photography: Jules Brenner. Editor: Carrol Sax. Original Music: Harry Sukman. Production Design: Mort Rabinowitz. Special Effects: Frank Torro. Associate Producer: Anne Cottle.

Ben Mears	David Soul
Richard Straker	James Mason
Mark Petrie	Lance Kerwin
Susan Norton	Bonnie Bedelia
Jason Burke	Lew Ayres
Barlow	Reggie Nalder
Bonnie Sawyer	Julie Cobb
Mike Ryerson	Geoffrey Lewis
Larry Crockett	Fred Willard
Chief Gillespie	Kenneth McMillan
Weasel Philips	Elisha Cook

Also: George Dzundza, Ed Flanders, Clarissa Kaye, Barney McFadden, Marie Windsor, Barbara Babcock, Bonnie Bartlett, Joshua Bryant, James Gallery, Robert Lussier, Brad Savage, Ronnie Scribner, Ned Wilson, James Gallery, Ernie Phillips, Joe Brooks.

that an arrival at New York City's Port Authority bus terminal would quickly lead to the bloodsucker's demise. But their dinner guest noted that one could drive through some of the small inland towns of Maine and never know if a soul was alive there. And so a bestseller was born.

'SALEM'S LOT centers on Ben Mears, a writer returning to his small New England hometown for the first time in many years. Ben hopes the journey will help him to work on a new project and resolve some inner questions born of his childhood experiences there. His book project is on the nature of pure evil and, like his personal doubts, the foreboding Marsten House seems to be at the center of both endeavors. The Marsten House and its history of depravity and corruption seems to hover like an ancient curse over 'Salem's Lot.

What Ben encounters, besides the love interest of a young teacher named Susan, is the incipient stages of a modern vampiric infestation being led by the undead Barlow and his human emissary, Straker. This vile, undead scourge is even more insidious than the dark, dreary, and, at times, bizarre secrets that grip the hearts and minds of most of the villagers (a frequent characteristic of small New England towns). Only Ben and a young boy named Mark seem able to recognize this situation for what it is. Will their efforts be enough to save 'Salem's Lot, or even themselves? Bloodletting ensues.

The theatrical adaptation of King's second novel had almost as many incarnations as a vampire has victims. 'Salem's Lot debuted on the NBC television network as a two-part, four-hour miniseries (200 minutes of footage) during 1979's November two-week "sweeps" period when the networks determine next year's advertising rates based on that period's ratings. The two installments were originally aired a full week apart. Reprise broadcasts found the two segments cut-and-spliced into a single three-hour MOW (movie of the week). King's vampire epic was subsequently re-edited further, into a two-hour version for European theatrical and domestic videocassette release. Though considerably shortened from its premiere length, this theatrical cut had material added to certain scenes, this being

> "Somebody said, 'What do you think Kubrick wants from THE SHIN-ING?' And I said, 'I think he wants to hurt people.' "
> —Speaking of The Shining with Christopher Evans

more graphic and violent than broadcast television would allow. Today, only the videocassette of this final revision is readily available, under the title 'Salem's Lot: The Movie.

Warner Bros. Pictures optioned King's 400-page vampire tome early in 1975, before the unexpected popularity of *Carrie*. Now envisioning a potential BIG HIT, it was taken for granted that a theatrical version would soon be forthcoming. But writer after writer failed to come up with an acceptable script. Stirling Silliphant (*Route 66*, *In the Heat of the Night*, *Village of the Damned*) was one of the first to try, eventually getting an executive producer's credit for his troubles. Robert Getchell (*Alice Doesn't Live Here Anymore*) had a go at it. Writer/director Larry Cohen (no relation to *Carrie* scripter Lawrence D. Cohen), the independent horror-monger responsible for the *It's Alive* series, also gave the project a stab. No one hit the mark. (This is one of reasons why it's common for only one in every ten scripts in active development to ever get made. A studio's annual abandonment costs for its stillborn projects often run into eight figures.)

Hoping that getting a director involved would help get the screenplay in shape, Warner approached just about every name director with a past horror association, including William Friedkin (*The Exorcist*) and George Romero (*Night of the Living Dead*). Still no dice. After two years of fruitless "development" the project was given over to Warner's television division, where it was taken over by Richard Kobritz, the creator of TV's popular *Peyton Place* series.

In 1978, Richard Kobritz had made, with director John Carpenter, *Someone Is Watching*, a suspenseful, above-average TV-movie. (The director immediately followed up with that pivotal slasher exercise, *Halloween*.) Kobritz swiftly went to work and Warners agreed to making the project into a miniseries. The three-and-a-half hour film would interest the networks and solve the problem of script length. Then Kobritz, after watching dozens of horror films, picked Tobe Hooper to direct. He was impressed by the filmmaker's first effort, the independently-made cult classic, *Texas Chainsaw Massacre*, and wanted 'Salem's Lot to eschew the usual bright and flat TV-movie "look." (Ironically, Hooper's name had been bruited about initially when the project was still at the theatrical division.)

Aware of the special limitations imposed by the small screen, the producer wanted to keep the camera constantly moving in order to build tension and a suspenseful atmosphere. He felt strongly that Hooper was just the man for the job. A Hollywood novice, the director's career was effectively dead in the water at the time. Hooper had been unable to find himself a suitable project, even after the wide industry attention *Chainsaw* had garnered for him. Trapped in a low-budget ghetto, *Eaten Alive* (1976) was the only picture the director had been able to complete, and he was just about to start *The Guyana Massacre* when Kobritz called.

Stephen King's first choice for screenwriter had been Richard Matheson, the science fiction and fantasy author often cited by King as a major influence in his work, especially in his shorter fiction. Indeed, Matheson's 1957 novel, I AM LEGEND, is a landmark of fantasy literature, transplanting traditional horror elements into a thoroughly modern setting for the first time in modern fiction. It is still a quite chilling account of a lone man, a hold-out, fighting for survival in suburban Los Angeles against legions of vampires. The novel has been filmed twice, as *The Last Man On Earth* (1964) and *The Omega Man* (1971). Matheson is currently the creative consultant on Spielberg's *Amazing Stories* TV series.

Carrie's producer, Paul Monash, took on the writing chores, turning in a script that pleased both Kobritz and King. Through careful construction of composite characters, the Emmy award-winning Monash molded a coherent narrative that could tell the story of 'Salem's Lot and still pass the scrutiny of the Standards and Practices people (the network's censors). With a European theatrical release already slated, footage with an extra dash of graphic intensity was shot for use in certain sequences, such as a close-up of Susan's father impaled on a rack of antlers. The foreign markets have since developed to such an extent that even the most innocuous TV-movie will routinely shoot "inserts" (usually nudity) exclusively for overseas release.

An active, creative producer (as opposed to simply a dealmaker), Kobritz decreed three major changes to King's material, all concerning the Barlow vampire. First, he didn't want another suave, smooth-talking *GQ*-type Prince of Darkness. Kobritz preferred an

> *"This bullshit about authors having their books changed. If you don't want to have that done, why'd you sell the goddamn thing in the first place? I love movies."*
> —Speaking of *Carrie* with Marty Ketchum, et al.

19

older personification of pure vampiric evil, such as first embodied by Max Schreck in *Nosferatu*, F.W. Murnau's 1922 classic (coincidentally, a similar vision was portrayed that same year by Klaus Kinski in Werner Herzog's remake). So, to be the mute but oh-so menacing Barlow, Kobritz hired his first choice, Reggie Nalder (the creepy villain in Hitchcock's 1956 production of *The Man Who Knew Too Much*). With Barlow more of a creature than a man, the role of Straker, the vampire's willing human servant, could be given much greater dimension.

Second, Kobritz wanted the inside of the Marsten House to reflect the decay and filth of the vampire's soul, rather than the immaculate cleanliness described in the novel. He liked the idea of the bizarre contrast between the always-immaculate Straker in his spotless tweed suit living in a rotting mansion that obviously had no working plumbing. Thirdly, it was essential that Barlow's coffin remain in the Marsten House basement for the final showdown between the forces of Good and Evil. This last point was for dramatic impact rather than literary logic—Eve's boarding house (used in the novel) just didn't have the same visual impact.

The project was budgeted at $4 million and filmed in 37 days, with Hooper shooting between 35-to-40 set-ups per day. (Not counting stunt work or special floor effects, an "average" feature usually takes 10-to-15 set-ups daily; less if you're Stanley Kubrick, more if you're Clint Eastwood.) Ferndale, California, near the Oregon border, doubled for Maine. The major interiors, such as the Marsten House set, were built on the soundstages of The Burbank Studios. Even so, a suitable false front had to be constructed at the Ferndale location in order for the Marsten House to look properly foreboding.

Levitating the vampires was handled rather ingeniously by using a camera crane and special body harness. By adding smoke

---

"My screenplay, which Kubrick chose not to use, was considerably different from the script that came out at his end. For one, my screenplay was pegged even more heavily than the book on something Kubrick never touch on: the past of the hotel. It says in 'Salems Lot, 'An evil house calls evil men.' That was the idea in THE SHINING. The hotel was not evil because those had been there, but those people went there because the place was evil."
—Speaking of *The Shining* with Christopher Evans

and shooting from directly front-on, the crane mechanism was hidden and the actor appeared to be floating without the aid of wires or post-production opticals. The trick of both shooting the scene and staging the action in reverse (running the camera backward but then projecting the film forwards) helped heighten the overall eeriness.

The response to the miniseries was mixed. The show's ratings were respectable, but many critics found the constricting parameters of television just too great a handicap for effective horror and nerve-shredding suspense. The Kobritz vision of Barlow was also not enthusiastically embraced in all quarters. Others found Hooper's direction to be lacking; a negative judgment since borne out by his efforts on *Lifeforce* (1985) and *Invaders From Mars* (1986).

But the late James Mason's classy performance as Straker was roundly cheered. Impressed by Monash's script, the noted British actor (also on the Kobritz "wishlist") readily agreed to do the role. As the vampire's erudite servant, his every phrase dripping with subtext (telling various townspeople how much Mr. Barlow will enjoy meeting them), Mason's rich characterization went a long way in offsetting David Soul's wimpoid writer, Ben Mears. (Mason's wife, Clarissa Kaye, also had a role, as Marjorie Glick.) Soul, formerly Starsky on television's *Starsky and Hutch*, had previously starred in *Little Ladies of the Night*, the highest rated TV-movie at that time. He has since gone on to greater things directing action shows for television, notably on *Miami Vice*.

As one might expect, the longer versions of *'Salem's Lot* contain additional character development and intrigue among the town's local color. Given the conventions of a vampire story, these extra moments with King's richly-drawn secondary characters could well be considered the very heart of the film. One significant difference in the longer broadcast versions is a matching prologue/epilogue framing device "bookending" the film. These sequences are placed in a tiny Central American village. They open with Mark and Ben in a darkened hut, their faces illuminated by a glowing vial of holy water. It can only mean one thing, the immediate proximity of loathsome undead creatures and a lengthy flashback explaining how such an awful mess got started some two years ago.

In the longest version, after we've learned how Ben and Mark had no choice but to turn 'Salem's Lot into 'Salem's Charcoal Pit, the narrative returns to our beleaguered pair preparing to face the approaching menace. We can easily guess that the town's shape-shifting survivors have long memories, life in the dead-lane being what it is. Sure enough, Ben is forced to confront none other than his former love interest, the pretty young Susan Norton, now a pretty young vampire. (Her new liquid diet must agree with her—all the other vampires looked like death warmed over.)

Refraining from joining his ex-sweetie in the perpetual nightlife and sharing Mark for dinner, the stalwart Ben stakes the hissing Susan-creature, but you know he doesn't really enjoy it. The writer turned vampire fighter then warns Mark that their job is not over yet. (Though a television series never did materialize from this obvious ploy, rumors of a *Return to 'Salem's Lot* keep arising).

Despite the fact that King had hoped for a big screen home for his novel, the writer seems to have been generally pleased with the results. He has stated that Paul Monash's screenplay was the only one to conquer the book's lengthy narrative. But like many, King questioned the mute representation and diminished presence of his vampire, as well as the week-long space between the two segments. He took particular exception to the handling of Susan's undead mien. Why was she able to retain her human beauty after two years of sleeping in dirt when the other characters looked totally wasted after just one day's sleep? "But keeping in mind the fact that was done as a TV-movie, I think it was done quite well," King told one reporter. ". . . *'Salem's Lot* could have turned out a lot worse than it did."

The author was reported to be relieved when the planned *'Salem's Lot* network series fell through. He had come to believe that broadcast television is just too institutionally fainthearted and unimaginative to handle real horror. But this was not to be King's last dealings with the electronic medium. □

"The idea for the hedge maze is Kubrick's and not mine. I had considered it, but then I realized it had been done in the movie THE MAZE [1953, directed in 3D by William Cameron Menzies the same year he did INVADERS FROM MARS] with Richard Carlson, and I rejected the maze idea for that reason. I have no knowledge as to whether or not Kubrick has ever seen that movie or if it happens to be coincidence."

—Speaking of *The Shining* with Bhob Stewart

THE SHINING

DIRECTED BY STANLEY KUBRICK

Wendy Torrance (Shelley Duvall) works up a head of scream worrying about husband Jack's writer's block.

THE SHINING (1980)

Would you believe that John Lennon inspired THE SHINING? Stephen King explains that the chorus to the Plastic Ono Band's anthemish "Instant Karma" had a telling effect on him. "The refrain went 'We all shine on.' I really liked that, and I used it." Indeed, his horror masterpiece was originally titled THE SHINE, but according to King he agreed to change it after a Doubleday executive told him,

Wendy has a heart-to-heart talk with junior (Danny Lloyd) about the house rules at The Overlook.

THE SHINING

A Warner Brothers release (The Producer Circle Group), 6/80. 143 minutes (R). Produced and Directed by Stanley Kubrick. Screenplay by Stanley Kubrick & Diane Johnson. Executive Producer: Jan Harlan. Director of Photography: John Alcott. Editor: Ray Lovejoy. Music: Bela Bartok, Krzysztof Penderecki, Gyorgy Ligeti. Conducted by Herbert Von Karajan. Original Music: Wendy Carlos & Rachel Elkin. Assistant Director: Brian Cook. Production Design: Roy Walker. Costumes: Milena Cononera. Make-up: Tom Smith.

Jack Torrance . . . . .Jack Nicholson
Wendy Torrance . . . . .Shelley Duvall
Danny Torrance . . . . .Danny Lloyd
Dick Hallorann . . . . .Scatman Crothers
Stuart Ullman . . . . .Barry Nelson
Delbert Grady . . . . .Philip Stone
Lloyd . . . . .Joe Turkel

Also: Anne Jackson, Tony Burton, Lia Beldam, Billie Gibson, Barry Dennen, David Baxt, Manning Redwood, Lisa Burns, Robin Pappas, Alison Coleridge, Burnell Tucker, Jana Sheldon, Kate Phelps, Norman Gay.

"You can't use that because it's a pejorative word for Black." Little did he know that an obnoxious avalanche of "ing" titles would soon pollute the horror field, on-screen and off (THE SEARING, *The Burning*).

Briefly, THE SHINING is King's variation on the venerable haunted house story, with loving nods to Shirley Jackson's THE HAUNTING OF HILL HOUSE and Richard Matheson's HELL HOUSE (both made into effective films, the former winning an Academy Award in 1963). Here, the Torrance family, Jack, Wendy and young Danny, are stuck in Colorado's Overlook Hotel, a rambling old building that closes for the winter due to its mountainous inaccessibility. Jack's been hired to caretake the deserted place, and he plans on using the peace and quiet to finally get that novel written. But what the elder Torrances don't realize is that the Overlook is a psychic magnet of corruption and evil, boasting a long history of general nastiness. Weak, reluctantly on the wagon, riddled by guilt and frustration, Jack Torrance gradually succumbs to the Overlook's murderous designs, designs centering on Danny's growing psychic abilities, his "shine." Madness ensues.

Written while King and his family were briefly living near Boulder, Colorado (King subscribes to the "write what you know" theory), THE SHINING was completed in only a few months. "I didn't know what was going to happen until the very end," the writer has stated. "That shows in the book. The original plan was for them all to die up there and for Danny to become the controlling force of the hotel after he died." But King found the results just too grim for his liking. He liked Danny Torrance too much to kill him off. "In the first draft of the book Jack beats his wife to death with the mallet and it was blood and brains and everything. It was really just terrible and I couldn't do it. I couldn't leave it that way."

A noted film industry analyst perceives the interaction of film and audience in terms of Expectation and Realization, readings on the E and R meters stuck somewhere behind our eyeballs. According to this theory, a person seeing a picture that delivers a poorer measurement of Realization than his pre-viewing Expectation level will be disappointed and badmouth the film; while someone having the same poor Realization level but who had no Expectations whatsoever would actually be satisfied with the viewing experience. Some films, especially sequels, generate such a high Expectation level that they can never successfully please their audience, resulting in poor word-of-mouth for what could have been, if judged without preconceptions, a perfectly wonderful movie.

One such picture was Stanley Kubrick's *The Shining*. And how could it not generate high expectations? First there was Stephen King's bestselling novel, a thrilling read. Added to this was director Stanley Kubrick, one of cinema's most creative and controversial filmmakers, having earned his place in the pantheon of motion picture geniuses with efforts such as *Dr. Strangelove*, *2001: A Space Odyssey*, and *A Clockwork Orange*. And then there was the film's star, Jack Nicholson, in his first major role since *One Flew Over the Cuckoo's Nest*. Talk about a high "want to see" level!

But Kubrick's vision of *The Shining* failed to generate much satisfaction for the mainstream audience, namely King's fans. Most just didn't find it the ultimate expression of horror they had hoped for. Some critics did hail it as a masterful examination of the disintegration of the family unit, or some such subtextual wonderment, their point being that *The Shining* was an "anti-horror" film.

This analysis is supported by the film's editing, which consistently operates against traditional horror film shock tactics (or "codes," according to those high-brow semiologists). Instead of keeping his camera in unsettling close-up on a dread-filled Wendy as she roams the Overlook only to have a drooling Jack Torrance suddenly jump into the frame accompanied by screaming violins, Kubrick repeatedly cuts away to show us Jack creeping up on her. Thus, the film's balloon of tension is continually deflated, eliminating that critical element of surprise.

King's theory on Kubrick's intention is that while the director "knew exactly where all the scares should go and where all the payoffs should come" he simply found this too easy and decided to abandon the genre "codes" for his own construction. Rational and pragmatic, Kubrick had trouble, according to King, even academically understanding the fears inherent in the existence of the supernatural world. An expatriate living and working in England, Kubrick would call up King at home in Maine, asking if ghost stories weren't essentially optimistic statements? Why people were scared of ghosts when the presence of spirits prove there was an afterlife?

Perhaps at the root of Kubrick's puzzlement was the fact, as he told King, that he did not believe in God, Hell, an afterlife, the Easter bunny or any of that other stuff. Thus, as King sees it, Kubrick abandoned the evil nature of the Overlook to focus instead at the character's internal evil, turning the film into "a domestic tragedy with only vague supernatural overtones. That was the basic flaw: Because he couldn't believe, he couldn't make the film believable to others."

Style over content, form over function, intellect over belief; whatever the case, most will agree that Kubrick's film is the most beautiful and stylish of the King adaptations.

But style and beauty don't come cheap, and Kubrick is known to be a fanatical perfectionist, a control freak who will go to any lengths to get the shot or performance he wants. The late Scatman Crothers, who played the pivotal role of the sympathetic cook Hallorann, recalled doing over twenty takes of a simple long shot where he gets out of a car and walks across the street. No dialogue, no other people involved, just stepping out of a car and walking across the street. The number of takes with actual speaking parts could run into the sixties.

The production design for that giant battery of evil, the Overlook Hotel, was based on an existing establishment in the Colorado Rockies. The magnificent aerial establishing shots utilized this location, being accomplished by MacGillvray/Freeman films, a Southern California-based firm then best known for having pioneered technically dazzling surfing films.

But the rest of the Overlook, including its snowbound exteriors, was constructed on huge soundstages at the Shepperton Studios near London. The largest and most intricate of their type, these sets

Snowbound: Scatman Crothers plows through the powder on his way to rescue Danny from the tender mercies of his father.

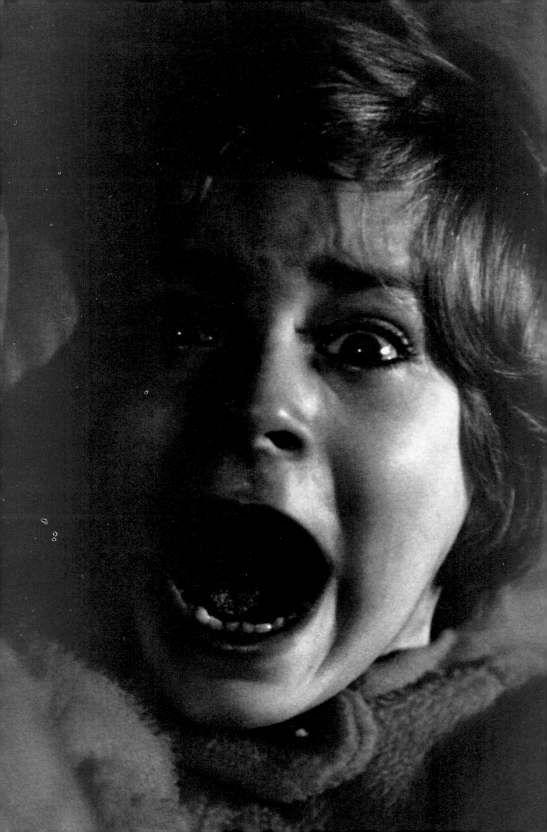

were designed to be totally "practical," meaning that all the lighting fixtures worked and there were no "wild" walls or false ceilings to facilitate camera booms and klieg lights. Banks of specially-wired lights supplied "daylight" through the set's windows. The interior lights were run by computerized dimmers, ensuring consistent exposure levels from shot to shot.

One of the reasons for this unusual set was Kubrick's planned use of the recently introduced Steadicam, an operator-worn camera mount first employed in the 1976 film, *Bound for Glory*. Built around battery-driven gyroscopes, the precision-balanced Steadicam (whose operator had to be rather strong and specially trained) could achieve incredibly fluid camera moves without relying on dolly tracks or boom mounts. Being able to closely follow the actors from room to room in long, uninterrupted takes brought a heretofore unseen immediacy to even the most mundane material. (It didn't take long for this innovation to become overused by lesser talents the film world over.)

Though used throughout the production of *The Shining*, the device was especially noticeable in the claustrophobic sequences of Danny Torrance running from his crazed father through the snowy (styrofoam chips and rock salt) hedge maze, and riding his Big Wheels through the hotel's haunted corridors. Garret Brown, the device's inventor and operator, was pushed along in a wheelchair in order to keep pace with the fast-peddling young actor.

Using a haunted hedge maze rather than recreating the novel's lethal topiary garden was just one of several basic changes co-scripter Kubrick brought to King's material. Interestingly, King has said that his original concept was in fact a maze, but he rejected the notion because he had seen it used in *The Maze*, a 1953 film directed in 3-D by William Cameron Menzies the same year he did the classic *Invaders from Mars*. (Menzies also executed the awesome sets for *The Thief of Bagdad* in 1924.) "The idea for the hedge maze is Kubrick's and not mine," King told one interviewer. "I have no knowledge as to whether or not Kubrick has ever seen that movie or if it happens to be coincidence."

As important as the production's complex sets and high-tech camera work, and perhaps the most intense overall element in the finished picture, was the disturbing soundtrack Kubrick laid over his images. Noted synthesizer wizard Wendy Carlos (once again working with Kubrick after *2001* and *A Clockwork Orange*) and Rachel Elkind composed an original and eerie title theme. And again relying on classical music, Kubrick also selected works by Bela Bartok (a radical classicist who often abandoned the traditional Western diatonic scale) and Polish composer Krzysztof Penderecki. Indeed, the soundtrack album of *The Shining* is one of the best ever put on vinyl.

Though never officially revealed, estimates on the budget for this elaborate production generally range between $11 and $18 million. Preproduction was unusually long. The sets took close to a year to construct and John Alcott, Kubrick's longtime cinematographer (portions of *2001*, all of *A Clockwork Orange* and *Barry Lyndon*) needed time for shooting tests with the complicated lighting systems. Additionally, the 17-week shooting schedule stretched to 27, largely due to cast and key personnel illness, and Jack Nicholson's recurring back problems.

The Shining opened to disappointing critical response and generally poor word-of-mouth. Additionally, the picture's 142-minute running time (Kubrick snipped four minutes after its premiere) allowed for only two evening shows instead of the standard three, a reduced "fill and spill" factor. So it's not surprising that *The Shining* didn't "break even" until its overseas runs, a truly poor outing for a film which boasted such major talents in front and behind the camera.

Stephen King still talks about wanting to eventually remake the picture. He also mentions his own script, one that he was contractually obliged to write. Kubrick reportedly refused to read it so that King's ideas wouldn't color the director's own creative palette. According to King, his screenplay departed from his novel by concentrating on the Overlook's legacy of evil and skipping Jack Torrance's job interview and his family life in Boulder. (Incidentally, King's first screenplay was not from one of his own works, but rather Ray Bradbury's influential fantasy classic, SOMETHING WICKED THIS WAY COMES.)

King has said of his own unseen *Shining* script, "It was pegged a lot more to the history of the hotel because I was really interested in the idea that an evil place calls evil men—which is a line from 'SALEM'S LOT. The screenplay that I wrote begins with total blackness on screen and the sounds of people talking. It turns out that these are Mafia hit men, and there are shotgun flashes and screams. Then this voice says, 'Get his balls.' There's another scream, then

Axe and ye shall receive: Wendy should have remembered to put out the "No Peddlers" sign.

you see the hotel."

Of Kubrick's effort, King is, like most people, generally disappointed. He cites Jack Nicholson as a prominent problem. Whether from Kubrick's intention or the fact that Nicholson's last major role had been in *Cuckoo's Nest*, his character seems crazy the minute he's first on the screen. Not much chance for a tragic and *gradual* descent into madness, the guy's already there! King also questions Kubrick's and co-screenwriter Diane Johnson's approach to the material, wondering how these two academics could hope to make an effective film from his horror novel when they knew nothing about the field and freely admitted to having no real respect for supernatural concepts. In short, they think too much and feel too little.

King has alternately characterized *The Shining* as "a live grenade which [Kubrick] heroically threw his body on," and "this great, big gorgeous car with no engine in it." □

CREEPSHOW

DIRECTED BY GEORGE ROMERO

Novelist as young thespian: Stephen King in "The Lonesome Death of Jordy Verrill" episode of Creepshow.

CREEPSHOW (1982)

These days every horror writer with any ambition wants to go to Hollywood and play the movie game. Though often an artistically barren and soul-crushing business which hungrily uses up people like human Kleenex, these writers still wanna be in pictures. Hey, who doesn't! The role most starry-eyed scribes use for entry is that of screenwriter, preferably adapting their own work. More often than not, they secretly harbor desires to go on to directing their material as well.

Clockwise from top left: George Romero, Hal Holbrook, Adrienne Barbeau, Carrie Nye, Viveca Lindfors, E.G. Marshall, Fritz Weaver, Leslie Nielsen.

CREEPSHOW

A Warner Brothers release (UFD/Laurel Entertainment), 10/82. 120 minutes (R). Directed by George Romero. Produced by Richard Rubinstein. Original Screenplay by Stephen King. Executive Producer: Salah M. Hussanein. Director of Photography: Michael Gornick. Editors: Michael Spolan ("Father's Day" & "Something's Creeping Up on You"), Pasquale Buba ("The Lonesome Death of Jordy Verrill"), George Romero ("Something to Tide You Over"), Paul Hirsh ("The Crate"). Original Music: John Harrison. Production Design & Scenic Special Effects: Cletus Anderson. Costume Design: Barbara Anderson. Make-up Special Effects: Tom Savini. Comic Book Art: Jack Kamen.

Upson Pratt	E.G. Marshall
Henry Northrup	Hal Holbrook
Wilma Northrup	Adrienne Barbeau
Dexter Stanley	Fritz Weaver
Richard Vickers	Leslie Nielsen
Sylvia Grantham	Carrie Nye
Aunt Bodelia	Viveca Lindfors
Hank Blaine	Ed Harris
Harry Wentworth	Ted Danson
Jordy Verrill	Stephen King

Also: Warner Shook, Robert Harper, Elizabeth Regan, Gaylen Ross, Jon Lormer, Dan Keefer, Bingo O'Malley, John Amplas, David Early, Nan Mogg, Iva Jean Saracini, Joe King, Christine Forrest, Chuck Aber, Cletus Anderson, Kate Karlowitz, Peter Messer, Marty Schiff, Tom Savini.

Just how many successfully make the bookwriter-to-screen-writer transition? Damn few, in or out of the horror genre. Science fiction thriller writer Michael Crichton made the leap to the big leagues with *The Andromeda Strain*, a hit novel he was able to adapt for the screen. It wasn't long before he was directing as well and, despite recent disappointments like *Runaway*, he's still fruitfully working within the system. Nicholas Meyer took this same route and was able to parlay his bestselling Sherlock Holmes pastiche, THE SEVEN PERCENT SOLUTION, into a Hollywood calling card. He went on to direct two well-received science fiction films, *Time After Time* and *Star Trek II: The Wrath of Kahn*, as well as the highly-rated post-nuclear war TV-movie, *The Day After*. Meyer is currently working on projects at Paramount.

Some older directors, such as Elia Kazan and Sam Fuller, were also successful novelists, but they were filmmakers first and foremost.

Leslie Nielsen discusses his favorite band, The Talking Heads, with sandman Ted Danson.

The time for marriage counseling has passed as Nielsen plots revenge on his unfaithful wife.

Stephen King never hides the fact that the genre films of the Fifties were a great influence on his work. Still a fan at heart, he often reviews or recommends current films that catch his fancy. His enthusiastic praise of the ultra-low budget shocker, *The Evil Dead*, was instrumental in getting the picture a domestic distribution deal. His comments were subsequently used in the picture's ad campaigns, which helped the picture find its audience.

It's not surprising that a partnership born of mutual admiration would develop between King and George Romero, the filmmaker responsible for the grisly and influential *Night of the Living Dead* (1967). This now-classic zombie picture (a disparate group of humans are besieged in a remote farmhouse by mysteriously re-animated corpses) was filmed in black & white 16mm for $127,000 (roughly half the cost of colorizing it for television 19 years later) and has grossed over $40 million worldwide. King and Romero first met during the great *'Salem's Lot* script search and they hit it off immediately. The two horror-meisters remained in touch after that project was long over, hoping to eventually work together if the right opportunity presented itself.

Writer-editor-cinematographer-director Romero never was successfully incorporated into the Hollywood system, although he

The corpses come home to roost when Danson and Gaylen Ross return from a quick dip in the ocean.

claims to have tried to launch projects there. The filmmaker remained in his Pittsburgh headquarters (a commercial and industrial film house) as a working independent—unencumbered by studio politics, but handicapped by the lack of significant funding. (Having been complete novice to the business side of filmmaking, Romero committed the costly error of not properly copyrighting *Night of the Living Dead*, allowing his film to fall into public domain and out of his financial control.)

After some missteps with various low-budget producers and distributors, Romero hooked up with neophyte producer Richard Rubinstein. Romero and Rubinstein formed Laurel Productions as a developing (or "preproduction") entity for feature projects. With financial help from Dario Argento, one of Italy's leading horror directors, they were able make the astonishing *Dawn of the Dead* in 1977. Romero's preeminence as a maker of uncommonly horrific films was decisively, if not violently, reestablished.

The second chapter in Romero's "living dead" trilogy, *Dawn of the Dead* (independently filmed for $3 million in the Pittsburgh area), led to a solid working relationship with United Film Distributors. UFD, an enterprise owned by the United Artist Theatre Circuit (not to be confused with the major theatrical releasing company,

United Artist Pictures), was willing to release the picture "unrated," a move that invariably results in the exhibitors giving the picture their own de facto X-rating. (It would have been rated X anyway for violence, and no major distributor has handled a film exceeding an R certification since Marlon Brando asked for the butter.)

Taking a limited number of prints around the country in a market-by-market releasing campaign, *Dawn of the Dead* grossed over $55 million for UFD. They quickly signed Laurel to a three-picture deal, the first of which was the ill-conceived *Knightriders* (1981). Close viewers of that film (those who can sit through it) will glimpse a brief cameo by Stephen and Tabitha King. This is King's first on-camera appearance, another manifestation of that infectious movie bug.

Once upon a time (so the story goes), when Romero and Rubinstein were in Maine visiting King, the author lined his un-optioned books on a shelf and asked Romero which he wanted. Romero picked THE STAND, a 900 + page epic. King then wrote a lengthy screenplay which called for a five-hour film, a nearly impossible concept to finance in America. (Many Soviet bloc films run four hours or longer, are shot in 70mm, and boast a cast of literally thousands—a benefit of state funding.) So King and Romero decided to first attempt another film project (or films, if need be) in order to raise money and credibility for *The Stand*. (Subsequent script adaptations by King first called for two two-hour films, then later for a single three-hour feature.)

"When Stanley Kubrick was gonna do THE SHINING, we were living in a little town in western Maine, and I was up one morning shaving my face and my wife came in. The phone had rung and she said, 'It's for you.' And I said, 'Well, who is it?' She said, 'Stanley Kubrick from London.' I had shaving cream over half my face and I just sort of picked up the phone and said, 'Stanley, how are you!' He wanted to talk about ghosts, and wasn't the horror story or the story of ghosts always fundamentally optimistic because it suggested that we went on afterward? And I said, 'Well it is, Stanley, but what if a person died insane and came back?' There was a long silence. And I also said, 'What about hell? What if there really is hell?' And Stanley said, 'I don't believe in that.' So I said, 'Well good, cool, do what you want.' "

—Speaking of *The Shining* at Bellerica Library

Thus was born *Creepshow.*

King opted to be directly involved in the writing and filmmaking process, making this the first time Romero allowed someone else to author one of his films. Early story concepts called for a series of horrific "black outs," short but shocking sequences similar to the *Lights Out* radio shows. Romero wanted five stories in five wildly different styles and with no linking device, changing film stock and frame dimensions and even using 3-D for one. Eventually this idea mutated into an anthology of short stories in the style of the classic horror comics of the Fifties—namely those published by E.C. Comics—beloved by both King and Romero.

The E.C. horror comics of the mid-Fifties were quite graphic yet often humorous tales (they were also highly moral, in a weird way), that led to the industry's self-regulating Comics Code Seal of Approval. This public relations move by the major comic publishers followed a series of McCarthy-like Congressional hearings into the comics industry. (Public outcry had been fueled by Dr. Frederick Wertham's sensationalistic book, THE SEDUCTION OF THE INNOCENT—which purported to establish a link between comic books like E.C.'s and juvenile delinquency.)

The seal of approval program succeeded in soothing the public, but the E.C. line was unable to flourish under the new arrangement. Nothing if not resourceful, E.C.'s publisher William Gaines skirted the board of review issue by entering the magazine field with the zany and satiric *Mad* magazine, originally a comic title he started at the end of the E.C. period. Ironically, the famed E.C. comics like *Vault of Horror, Tales from the Crypt* and *Weird Science* are today prized collectors' items and have been reprinted in deluxe, high-quality editions. Like the horror and science fiction films of the period, these comics with their colorful history influenced both King and Romero. Thus they returned to this era for inspiration.

In sixty days King completed a script containing five individual episodes and a framing story. The framing device opens with a stern father who is angered and alarmed over his son's choice of reading material—a *Creepshow* comic book. He angrily pitches the offending literature into the garbage can. That night a skeletal figure (The Spectre) directs our attention to the comic's pages blowing in the wind. The comic's "splash" (pictorial) title pages segue into live-action, becoming one of the film's chapters: "Father's Day," "The Lonesome Death of Jordy Verrill" (adapted from King's previously published story, "Weeds"), "The Crate" (also an adaptation), "Something to Tide You Over," and "They're Creeping Up on You." The film's framing device concludes afterward with the son using voodoo to get even with his narrow-minded dad, while trash collectors haul away the comic. Romero would film the picture almost entirely as it was first written. King was on hand to make any overnight script changes as needed, including alternate dialogue for the "television safe" version required by broadcasters.

Despite the fact that since their heyday in the Thirties and Forties, anthology-structured films have never made money at the domestic box office, UFD approved Romero's $8 million budget, his biggest ever. (In Europe, the anthology format remained popular well into the Sixties and British producer Milton Subotsky had already made two films directly adapting stories from the E.C. comics.) Accustomed to working in the Pittsburgh area with his regular non-union crew, Romero's hefty production budget would allow him the heretofore unknown luxury of an ample shooting schedule and name actors.

King and Romero came up with a wishlist of actors and were able to get most of them, including Viveca Lindors, E.G. Marshall, Leslie Nielsen, Ted Danson, Hal Holbrook, Adrienne Barbeau and Fritz Weaver. Rounding out the cast was Stephen King himself, assaying the role of hayseed Jordy Verrill at the invitation of director Romero. This reflects Romero's homegrown working methods, having assembled over the years a virtual ensemble company of regular players and production staff who are free to jump from job to job. Soundtrack composer John Harrison, for example, doubled as the film's first assistant director. Other sometime members of the Romero troupe include make-up artist and actor Tom Savini, director of photography (now turned director) Michael Gornick, and such actors as Ed Harris and Warner Shook (from *Knightriders*), and Gaylen Ross (*Dawn of the Dead*).

King's 8-year old son, Joe, was cast as the put-upon kid whose comic book starts the film in motion. Cheerfully admitting his role in the exploitation of his son, King has said that the experience was at first unsettling for the youngster, but when the pressure was put on, Joe went to work instead of freaking out.

Special make-up effects artist Tom Savini has become a cult figure to fans of movie gore, especially after working on *Friday the 13th*. He can be seen in *Creepshow* as one of the garbagemen at the

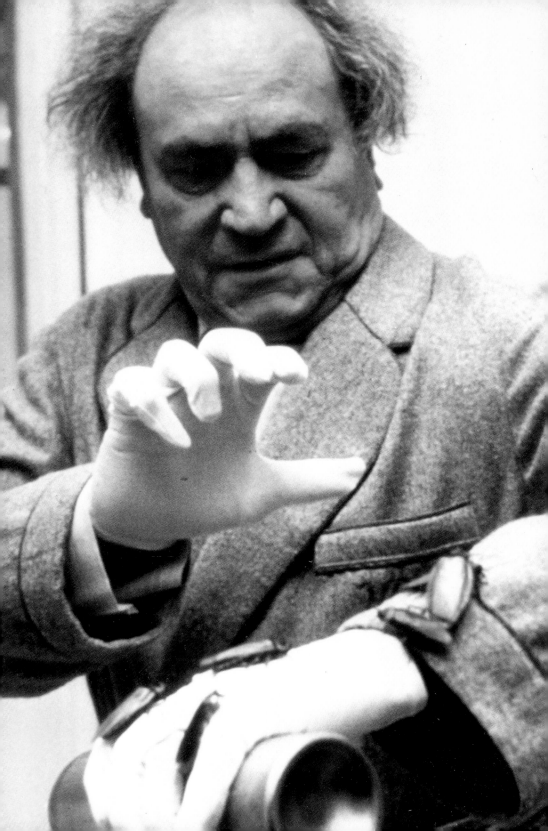

picture's end. Savini had a featured role in *Knightriders* and has recently starred in a low-budget direct-to-video feature, *The Slasher*.

Further emulating his source material, Romero consciously replicated the E.C. comics visual style. He heightened the more intense scenes with dramatic camera angles, saturated the frame with garish primary colors, and even put halo-like "shock" lines around his characters in selected close-ups. The film's emotional tone was one of grotesque black humor and shocking terror, the kind induced by good old fashioned monsters and supernatural weirdness—not maniacal killers slashing up sexually active teenagers. While the slobbering creatures and gushing blood effects one expects in a Romero film are indeed present, their graphic qualities are partially mitigated by Romero's stylized cinematography and King's tongue-in-cheek screenplay. Romero originally intended to score the film in using "stock" library music, as he had done with *Night of the Living Dead*. However, John Harrison's evocative synthesizer score gave the director a greater degree of flexibility and superior sound quality.

Creepshow debuted in France at the Cannes Film Festival and ran 129 minutes. The response was very positive and UFD was able to begin selling off foreign rights to different European distributors. (Despite the prestigious awards, Cannes is little more than a trade show in disguise.) More favorable word of mouth was engendered by a rave review in the trade paper, *Variety*. Warner Bros. ultimately "picked up" the feature from UFD for domestic distribution, ensuring a much wider release and better theatre bookings and terms (and more prompt exhibitor payments). With the high-profile elements of King and Romero as well as the positive word of mouth the picture had already generated, Warners had big plans for picture. They worked out a merchandising tie-in with the 7-11 stores and rescheduled the film's summer release for a more timely induced Halloween release. They also prevailed on Romero to trim the picture's running time down to a more exhibitor-pleasing 2 hours.

Having a tie-in movie edition published is another popular promotional and merchandising tool used by film marketeers. Warner wanted a *Creepshow* novelization from King but he rejected that plan immediately, having refused similar proposals in the past. The writer preferred keeping to the spirit of the film's conceptual origins by putting out an actual *Creepshow* comic book instead. Warner agreed. Previously, King had worked with master horror artist Berni Wrightson (also an E.C. fan) on a limited edition project entitled THE

CYCLE OF THE WEREWOLF. At King's behest, Wrightson was duly commissioned, with King himself handling the text and continuity for the glossy comic book. (King had earlier enjoyed scripting one of his short stories, "The Lawnmower Man," for Marvel Comics.) Veteran E.C. artist Jack Kamen, a friend of the Rubinstein family, created Laurel's original pre-release poster as well the artwork for the *Creepshow* comic featured in the film.

Despite Warner's best efforts, *Creepshow* did not play well after its initial weekend. Most horror films are prey to this pattern, experiencing quick declines in attendance during their second week. In this case, the decline was a precipitous plummet. The teenage audience didn't know or care about the old E.C. comics and were perhaps put off by the picture's campy elements. Mixing horror and humor is at best a tricky endeavor. The critical response was also far below expectations, though some responded to individual segments like "The Crate" or "They're Creeping Up on You."

The Stand still awaits production, but continues being listed by Laurel as a project in development. PET SEMATARY, King's grim novel of resurrection through supernatural means, is also a Laurel property awaiting the green light. (King's *Pet Sematary* screenplay has made the rounds in Hollywood.) Currently filming, however, is *Creepshow II*, based on five more King short stories. This time Romero has scripted and cinematographer Michael Gornick is directing. □

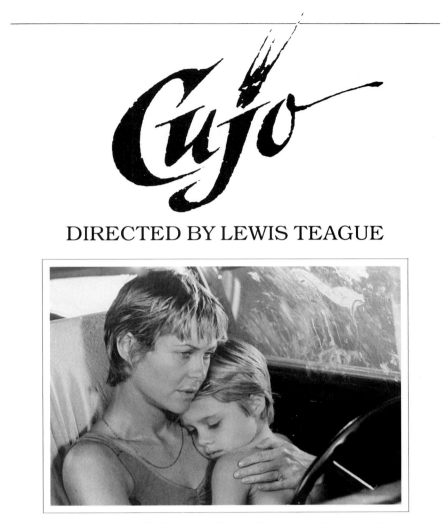

Cujo

DIRECTED BY LEWIS TEAGUE

Exhausted, Dee Wallace and Danny Pintauro take a rest break while Cujo readies another assault.

CUJO (1983)

1983 saw no less than three Stephen King-derived films on the market. *Cujo* was unleashed in the summer, *Dead Zone* just in time for Halloween, and *Christine* peeled out for Thanksgiving. What makes this copious cinematic crop even more amazing is that all three are very entertaining. Two of them could actually be consid-

Pass the Sominex: Danny Pintauro spends a restless night in the shadowy grip of fear.

CUJO

A Warner Brothers release (Taft Entertainment), 6/83. 120 minutes (R). Directed by Lewis Teague. Produced by Daniel H. Blatt & Robert Singer. Screenplay by Don Carlos Dunaway & Lauren Currier. Associate Producer: Neil A. Machlis. Director of Photography: Jan De Bont. Editor: Neil Travis. Original Music: Charles Bernstein. Production Design: Guy Comtois. Makeup Special Effects: Peter Knowlton. Animal Action Director: Karl Lewis Miller

Donna Trenton . . . . .Dee Wallace
Victor Trenton . . . . .Daniel Hugh-Kelly
Steve Kemp . . . . .Christopher Stone
Joe Camber . . . . .Ed Lauter
Charity Camber . . . . .Kaiulani Lee
Brett Camber . . . . .Billy Jacobi
Tad Trenton . . . . .Danny Pintauro

Also: Mills Watson, Sandy Ward, Jerry Mardin, Merritt Olsen, Arthur Rosenberg, Terry Donovan-Smith, Robert Elross, Robert Behling, Clair Nons, David H. Blatt.

ered quite good films, regardless of their King-ly origins.

Cujo, a four-legged Jaws: Donna Trenton and her six-year-old son, Tad, are trapped for several harrowing days in their broken-down Pinto—continually menaced by the rabid St. Bernard of the film's title. Dehydration ensues.

Actually, CUJO is more a story of domestic strife, Castle Rock style. Having fallen into a "bored housewife" syndrome, Donna Trenton is trying to get her life back together and break off a depressing, adulterous affair with local layabout Steve Kemp. Her husband, Vic, has problems of his own: his small advertising agency is in a crisis mode following the disastrous introduction of a new kids' cereal by their biggest client. On top of all this, young "Tadder" is having night fears: convinced that a monster lives in his closet.

Outside of town, the Camber family pounds their way through rural life. Joe Camber fixes cars, drinks beer and insults his wife, usually all at once. Charity Camber keeps house and tries to figure out how to get Joe's permission to take their son Brett on a one-way visit to her relatives in another state. And Brett's St. Bernard, Cujo, has just been bitten by a rabid bat.

Like a daytime drama, it's not long before these two tales of domestic troubles intersect. Steve resents Donna dumping him. He trashes her house. Vic discovers his wife's infidelity, but has to deal with his business crisis out of town. Charity buys a winning lottery ticket. She uses the money to buy Joe an engine hoist and herself and Brett a vacation to her sister's. Brett notices Cujo acting a bit strange but, afraid that his father will make him stay home if his dog is sick, he doesn't mention it to Joe.

And the Trenton family Pinto can barely make it up the hill to

> "One day at their summer camp, or whatever it was, a story circu-
> lated that a dog had been hit by a train and the dead body was on
> the tracks. These guys are saying, 'And you should see it man, it's all
> swelled up and its guts are falling out and it's [real] dead. I mean it's
> just as dead as you ever dreamed of anything being dead.' And you
> could see it yourself, just walk down these tracks and take a look at
> it, which they did. George said, 'Someday I'd like to write a story
> about that,' but he never did. He's running a restaurant now, a great
> restaurant."
> —Speaking of Stand By Me at Bellerica Library

A tender moment for Wallace and lover Steve Kemp is no protection against the dog day afternoon.

the Cambers' place for some much-needed servicing. Hey, is anybody home?

Reportedly, King sold CUJO to the small Taft International production company because he liked *The Boogens*, a wonky, low-budget feature they put out in 1981. He also suggested Lewis Teague for the directing chores. "I think this guy is the most unusual film director in America," King told horror writer Charles L. Grant. "You never hear his name brought up at parties. Teague did *The Lady in Red* and *Alligator*. He also did a picture called *Fighting Back*. He has absolutely no shame and no moral sense. He just wants to go get ya and I relate to that!"

Despite King's enthusiastic endorsement, director Peter Medak (*The Changeling*) was hired instead. Medak brought in Barbara Turner to rewrite King's screenplay (something most directors do as a matter of course).

The $5 million production set up shop in Northern California's Mendocino County, which doubled for King's Maine countryside as it had in *'Salem's Lot*. But Medak, according to King, just couldn't get a leash on the project and left the production ("ankled" in Hollywood's colorful vernacular) after one day's shooting. Lewis Teague was suddenly called in as a pinch-hit director, not an enviable position. He immediately brought in *his* writer, Don Carlos Dunaway, to fix what he felt were weaknesses in the script. In Teague's view, the biggest flaw was young Tad's death after Cujo's lengthy siege.

This conclusion to Donna and her son's ordeal has bothered King ever since he completed the novel. To hear him tell it, the writer never intended to have little Tadder kick off. But in the process of ending the book King "discovered" that the child did indeed die. "Hey, I'm sorry, sometimes kids die. I couldn't help it."

Teague believed that after putting the characters and audience through a cinematic version of the ordeal in the Pinto, to have Tad end up a fatality was just too much of a downer. King realizes that movies are subject to different conventions than the literary experience and was delighted with the change. He felt that fans would now have the luxury of choosing which version they preferred. "This bullshit about authors having their books changed," King told an interviewer. "If you don't want to have that done, why'd you sell the Goddamn thing in the first place? I love movies."

King has described his initial screenplay as "pretty good, it was not as faithful to the book as was the final result." According to King, Taft International wanted his name on the film, feeling that screen credit would help at the box office. "I think that they might've been right," the writer conceded later. Producers, however, cannot dictate

Cujo washes Wallace's windows with his tongue, but she's not appreciative in the least.

"*Go ahead—make my day!*" *Ms. Wallace displays Donna Trenton's maternal instincts in the face of canine terror.*

writing credits if they are signatories to the Writers Guild of America standard contractual agreements (and almost every company is). One of the agreement's provisions is to have the WGA review board arbitrate screen credits when disputes arrive. (The WGA has an inscrutable arcane formula for divining such things.) This arrangement not only protects WGA members but can save producers quite a few headaches as well.

Taft duly submitted the *Cujo* script to the Guild as "Screenplay by Stephen King." Barbara Turner immediately lodged a protest with the Guild. The Guild wrote to King, asking for a response to her protest and proposing a split, three-way credit. "They sent me a copy of the final screenplay which I read over, and I saw a lot of my stuff still in there," King has been quoted saying. "But at the time that the thing reached me I was in England doing a promotional round for

CHRISTINE and I didn't want to fight about it." Without a timely objection from King in the matter, the Guild gave the film a split-credit between Lauren Currier (Barbara Turner's pseudonym) and Don Carlos Dunaway.

Dee Wallace (*E.T., The Howling*) played Donna Trenton, with her real-life husband, Christopher Stone, as her illicit lover, Steve Kemp. The couple also paired in *The Howling* and Wallace now bills herself as Dee Wallace-Stone. Danny Pintauro was chosen over 200 other child actors to play Tad. Five different St. Bernards portrayed Cujo.

Transforming the lovable pooch into a marauding, fever-driven four-legged demon was accomplished by a variety of means. As well as the five "Cujo" dogs performing various stunts, mechanical dog heads were employed for some of the close-up, on-cue viciousness. One difficult stunt effect was executed using a man in a dog suit. Cujo's mangy maniacal mien was evoked through liberal amounts of red dye, foam and make-up mud. As you well know, canine actors are at their freshest early in the morning and late in the afternoon. And while human actors can stand around all day blocking out a scene, you must only rehearse a dog until he knows his part—he'll soon get bored and uncooperative. And don't forget to make sure that the caterer's truck parks downwind from the set!

The production's primary sequences took eight weeks to shoot and utilized all existing locations. Since Tad's bedroom had to appear normal by day but terrifying at night, a special set was constructed in a nearby warehouse to facilitate unusual camera angles.

The film's unpretentious intensity was generally well-received, even without the production flash of *The Shining* or the grotesque obsessiveness of *Carrie*. Dispatching the soap opera narrative elements with welcome economy, director Teague was able to create a grueling final third without resorting to cheap shocks or pointless gore. The entire picture, despite its storyline differences, is actually one of the truest in spirit to King's work.

Distributed by Warner Bros., *Cujo* opened quite well for a low-budget shocker competing with bigger pictures for a share of the summer market (but then again, there are far more people going to the movies during the summer). The picture took in $6 million in box office its first weekend and eventually made its "break even" figure of $20 million in domestic gross receipts.

King was also quite pleased with the film. "It's one of the scariest things you'll ever see," he stated. "It's terrifying!" □

DIRECTED BY DAVID CRONENBERG

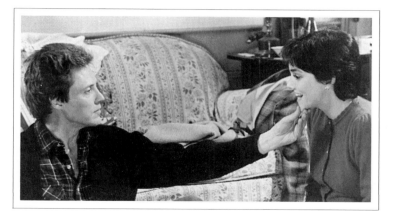

Johnny Smith (Christopher Walken) communes with ex-finacee Sarah Bracknell (Brooke Adams) in The Dead Zone.

THE DEAD ZONE (1983)

Though labeled a horror writer by the public and media, King disputes this blanket categorization. "FIRESTARTER, CARRIE and THE DEAD ZONE are all science fiction, in other words, they're not novels about ghosts, vampires or ghouls," he said on one occasion.

THE DEAD ZONE, Stephen King's 1979 bestseller, tells the tragic story of Johnny Smith, a nice guy from New Hampshire. His normal, average life is destroyed when a car crash puts him in a

Sarah and Johnny remembering the good old days, before Johnny's mind-altering accident.

THE DEAD ZONE

A Paramount Pictures release, 10/83. 103 minutes (R). Directed by David Cronenberg. Produced by Debra Hill. Screenplay by Jeffrey Boam. Executive Producer: Dino De Laurentiis. Associate Producer: Jeffrey Chernov. Director of Photography: Mark Irwin. Editor: Ronald Sanders. Original Music: Michael Kamen. Production Design: Carol Spier. Special Effects Cooridinator: John Belyeu. Costume Designer: Olga Dimitrov.

Johnny Smith . . . . Christopher Walken
Sarah Bracknell . . . . Brooke Adams
Greg Stillson . . . . Martin Sheen
Sheriff Bannerman . . . . Tom Skerritt
Dr. Sam Weizak . . . . Herbert Lom
Henrietta Dodd . . . . Colleen Dewhurst
Frank Dodd . . . . Nicholas Campbell
Roger Stuart . . . . Anthony Zerbe
Herb Smith . . . . Sean Sullivan
Vera Smith . . . . Jackie Burroughs

Also: Geza Kovacs, Robert Weiss, Simon Craig, Peter Dvorsky, Julie-Ann Heathwood, Barry Flatman, Raffi Tchalikian, Kenneth Pogue, Gordon Jocelyn, Bill Copeland, Jack Messinger, Chapelle Jaffe, Cindy Hines, Helene Udy, Ramon Estevez, Joseph Damenchini, Roger Dunn, Wally Bondarento, Claude Rae, John Koensgen, Les Carlson, Jim Bearden, Hardee Lineham, William Davis, Sierge LeBlanc, Vera Winiouski, John Kopnaiko, Dave Rigby, Cathy Scorsese.

coma for five years. He awakens, partially crippled, to find his fiancee, Sarah, married and his future plans as badly wrecked as his VW bug. Johnny is still bedridden when he discovers that his head injuries left him with more than a coma. He now has the double-edged gift of precognition. Touching a person or personal article puts Johnny into a vision of that person's life—where they came from, where they're going, even giving him information about their manner of death. How does Johnny, the ex-school teacher now tutoring students in a small town in Maine, deal with his peculiar "talent"? And how does society react to a man who can truly predict your future, divine your darkest secrets?

King often employs this "what if" technique to get a new project going. He told one interviewer, "What always happens for me, with a book, is that you frame the idea of, or the 'what if,' and little by little characters will take shape. Generally as a result of a secondary decision about the plot."

Johnny Smith copes as best he can with his unwanted precognitive abilities. He saves the life of one of his students and helps police catch the "Castle Rock Killer," a rape-murderer protected by the killer's own mother. Yet each time Johnny helps someone he's treated like a freak, either idolized or despised, forever an outcast.

But Johnny Smith is not THE DEAD ZONE's only "visionary." Good ol' boy Greg Stillson is rapidly becoming a very viable third party Presidential candidate. His seductive brand of conservative populism, holy roller campaign style and thug-like dealings with various political power brokers is reminiscent of Broderick Crawford's Willie Stark in *All the King's Men*. Stillson is a driven, paranoid psychopath with a Messiah complex. Through parallel narratives, King portrays two types of "prophets," Greg Stillson and Johnny Smith, poles apart but fated to meet.

Their paths cross at a local campaign rally: Stillson pumps Johnny's hand as he wades through the cheering crowd. What Johnny "sees" while touching the deranged politician is nothing less than World War III—Stillson launching a nuclear first-strike against Russia. How will Johnny deal with this knowledge? Should he attempt to save a society that continually ostracizes him? Premonitions ensue.

"I'm not afraid of that spiraling down into a very unpleasant conclusion," King has stated when discussing the book. "Partly because I think life sometimes does that, and also because I was really impressed by the American naturalists and the British naturalists when I was in high school and college. People like Thomas Hardy, Theodore Dreiser and Frank Norris." (These three writers are not exactly O. Henry or James Thurber.)

THE DEAD ZONE's book-to-film transformation began in 1981. Lorimar Productions was attempting to parlay their wildly profitable television expertise into similar achievement in beckoning theatrical venues. Having optioned King's book, Lorimar's Carol Baum contacted David Cronenberg during the early stages of the project's development. The Canadian writer-director was well known for his earlier science-gone-too-far horror films like *They Came from Within* and *Rabid*, but had yet to score major critical and commercial successes (which he would do with *Scanners* and *Videodrome*).

But before talks with Cronenberg began in earnest, other parties at Lorimar signed American director Stanley Donen. Filmmaker Sydney Pollack was named to produce. Donen had made his mark in Hollywood with a series of successful musicals (*Singin' in the Rain*, *Seven Brides for Seven Brothers*, *On the Town*). In the Sixties he moved on to more sophisticated projects like *Charade*, *Arabesque*, *Two for the Road*, and *Bedazzled*, before stumbling in the Seventies with *Lucky Lady* and *Saturn 3*. A formidable talent in his own right, Sydney Pollack is best known for *The Yakuza*, *Tootsie* and, now, *Out of Africa*.

Screenwriter Jeffrey Boam, whose only previous credit had been co-scripting Ulu Grosbard's *Straight Time*, was hired to adapt King's novel under Donen's supervision. The screenwriter thought the book was "longer than it needed to be," that it tended to ramble into subplots and was unnecessarily episodic. He saw the story's theme as depicting moral responsibility thrust upon decent people, and how this unwelcome moral charge is dealt with. Johnny Smith at first shuns this responsibility, but then ultimately sacrifices himself to it after shaking hands with the pathological Stillson.

Boam discarded King's Smith/Stillson parallel narratives, con-

---

"In fact, a lot of the novels I've written are really science fiction. 'Firestarter,' 'Carrie' and 'The Dead Zone' are all science fiction, in other words they're not novels about ghosts, vampires and ghouls."
—Speaking of *The Dead Zone* with Edwin Pouncey

centrating on Smith: his accident, recuperation, consequent powers, and how Johnny is compelled to use those powers—culminating in the Castle Rock Killer incident and finally his discovery of Stillson's future (if left unchecked). Boam's script capped these actions with a radical departure from King's book, a "shocker" scene in the hospital with Johnny, Sarah (now a Stillson campaign worker), Herb (Johnny's father), and Frank Dodd, aka The Castle Rock Killer. Unlike the book, in Boam's script Johnny's work with the police does not lead to Dodd's suicide. Instead, the killer is sent to an institute for the criminally insane—but not before he vows to get even with Johnny for tracking him down. Leaving for his rendezvous with Stillson, Johnny learns that Dodd has escaped. Johnny goes ahead with his assassination plan and is badly wounded.

Boam's climactic scene is in the hospital afterward, where Johnny lies dying while Sarah and Herb watch over him. When it gets late, Herb sends Sarah home. After a farewell kiss, we see Sarah leave Johnny's bedside and go down to the dark and spooky hospital garage. Sure enough, Frank Dodd is there with a big knife and he proceeds to hack up Sarah. With his last strength, Johnny whispers "garage" to Herb, who gets the hint and, too late, follows Sarah to the

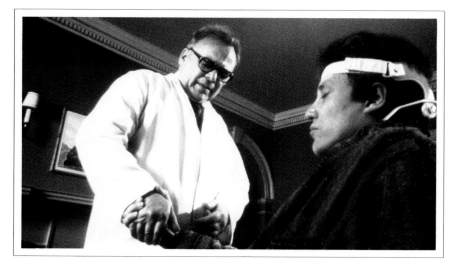

Future shake: Dr. Sam Weizak (Herbert Lom) presses the flesh to test Johnny's prophetic powers.

garage.

Now the kicker is that we've seen not Sarah's murder, but Johnny's *vision* of it, triggered when she kissed him goodbye. Herb arrives just as Dodd jumps from the shadows and one last tragedy is averted.

The reaction to this trick coda was less than positive. Cronenberg characterized it as "a direct rip-off of *Dressed to Kill*." King concurred. Dino De Laurentiis found the screenplay overly complicated, and went looking for new writers.

How had Dino gotten involved? He simply picked up the property from Lorimar after their excursion from the small screen to the silver screen proved disastrous. Lorimar's initial slate of pictures, with ironically prophetic titles like *Cruising*, *Fast Walking*, and *Looking to Get Out*, were box office poison—and the company discreetly retreated from the theatrical arena. (Later, as Lorimar-Telepictures, they would buy the venerable MGM backlot and production facilities from Ted Turner, signaling the end of one of Hollywood's most glamorous studios.)

De Laurentiis wasted no time in commissioning a screenplay from King. The novelist's version reportedly stayed close to the often bloody events in the book. Now the Castle Rock Killer was a more central character, and the script's opening scene showed Stillson in his back room, torturing a teenager. But Johnny's youthful past, partially explaining the genesis of his powers, was never touched on.

King says that De Laurentiis found the script too complex, while Boam felt the author was simply a better novelist than screenwriter, often the case when fiction writers work in Hollywood. (William Faulkner and Raymond Chandler are only two prime examples.) Boam contended that King had missed the essence of his own book, mistaking violence for theme. Whatever the reason, a series of new writers was hired, including Paul Monash (remember him?) and Andre Konchalavsky, a Soviet director whose Russian-language screenplay had to be translated into English, and then into Italian for De Laurentiis.

Around this same time, independent producer Debra Hill was brought in to oversee the project's development. Having cut her teeth on low-budget features with director John Carpenter, Hill had previously worked for De Laurentiis on two *Halloween* sequels. A stern taskmaster with fine sense of story, Hill was adept in getting pic-

The fire this time: Johnny accurately predicts that he should have worn flame-retardant pajamas to bed.

tures made on time and on a profitable budget. (She is currently working on a third *Halloween* installment at another studio.)

Hill ran into Cronenberg during a visit to John Landis's office on the Universal lot. The meeting resulted in the director being offered *The Dead Zone.* Still in postproduction with *Videodrome,* Cronenberg readily accepted. He had been interested in the project since the Lorimar days but he was not willing to work with another writer's screenplay. (Cronenberg usually writes and directs his own films. *The Dead Zone* would be the second exception to this rule.)

The director didn't bother reading the Russian screenplay and he rejected King's effort as well, not wanting to open his picture with a youngster being brutalized without motivation. It was decided that Cronenberg, Hill and Boam would brainstorm together and reshape the *original* screenplay into something all parties, including De Laurentiis, would be happy with. King has termed their efforts "a pretty decent script."

It took Hill, Cronenberg and Boam three days in a Toronto (Cronenberg's base) hotel to reconstruct the script. Hill also insisted on using storyboards to map out the script's several special effect sequences. (Storyboards are a series of literal diagrams of the scenic action, much like a comic book [and often done by former comic artists]. When used correctly, they can help control costs and keep the production on schedule, especially when planning elaborate, large-scale scenes, special effects and animation. Though preproduction paintings have been around since the silent days, Hitchcock was the first live-action director to use storyboards extensively.)

Cronenberg felt that storyboards would be counterproductive to his mercurial working methods, but he acquiesced nonetheless. *The Dead Zone* would be Cronenberg's first full-fledged major studio release (Paramount was distributing), and it might raise him from the status of a cult *auteur* (more critic-speak for "filmmaker"). A visual director who preferred to use action in telling a story rather than dialogue, Cronenberg switched the focus of the Donen-helmed script. The director wanted to bring Johnny Smith's prophetic visions to the foreground, accessing the story through Johnny's personal viewpoint, unlike the original script which saw the story's drama more objectively. Boam's "trick" hospital sequence was dropped. The book's final scene of Sarah crying at Johnny's graveyard was relocated to the amusement park where Johnny is first seen courting Sarah. (This brief coda is not in the final film, though King saw it in a rough cut. "It was all very pointless," summed up his

Pursuing a chilly new career in tunnel inspection and maintenance, Johnny checks for frozen forest rangers.

The grisly scene of the crime awaits Johnny on his rounds as he applies his clairvoyant powers to righting wrongs.

opinion of the scene. Cronenberg's last three pictures have all had brief codas that were later excised from the final version.)

Cronenberg also rethought the novel's "dead zone" concept. This referred a growing brain tumor that caused a black area, or "hole," and prevented Johnny from seeing his own fate within the psychic vistas. Feeling that this concept was not visually adequate, Cronenberg made the "dead zone" more metaphorical, having each successive visionary episode take a drastic toll on Johnny's health.

Though the final script kept only a few of the book's incidents and central concepts, Cronenberg felt it was very true to the spirit of King's work. (In fact, the novelist reportedly felt that some changes, such as reducing Johnny's tutorial student from a spoiled 18-year-old teenager to a vulnerable 11-year-old boy, as well as jeopardizing him at a hockey pond instead of the book's gymnasium fire, were not only acceptable to him but an improvement on his material.)

Being a small "mini-major," De Laurentiis is able to be more supportive of his filmmaker's wishes than the typical Hollywood studio. But the knowledgeable producer (then setting up shop in his North Carolina studios) did have some non-negotiable guidelines for *The Dead Zone*. One was cast approval for the major roles, the other that the screenplay must be finalized before entering principal photography. Used to creating his own projects, David Cronenberg often rewrites drastically during the course of production, even improvising scenes on the soundstage. *Videodrome*, his previous picture, had started shooting without a completed script, which some feel contributes to the picture's ultimately unsatisfactory conclusion.

The final screenplay was completed in November of '82. Budgeted at $10 million, production began the following January on soundstages in Toronto and 40 miles away in Niagara-on-the-Lake for the New Hampshire locations. Cronenberg's regular production crew was on board, including cinematographer Mark Irwin, assistant director John Board and art director Carol Spier. For the "look" of the film, Cronenberg referenced the now-iconic work of Norman Rockwell. He was taken by the revered artist's naive and nostalgic rendering of mid-America and it's no mistake that the Stillson campaign posters look like Rockwell imitations.

The part of Johnny Smith was originally to be played by Nicholas Campbell, the star of Cronenberg's *The Brood*. The director's first choice for the role of Castle Rock's sheriff was Hal Holbrook, an actor unfamiliar to De Laurentiis, but who would later feed his wife to a monster in *Creepshow*. Tom Skerritt (*Alien*) eventually got the sheriff's part and Campbell ended up playing Frank Dodd, the Castle Rock Killer. Interestingly, King's own first choice for Johnny Smith's character was comic actor Bill Murray (*Ghostbusters*). "Dino thought it was a good idea," the writer said in an interview. "But for whatever reason, Murray couldn't do it and De Laurentiis eventually signed Christopher Walken (*The Deer Hunter*) for the lead role." Once Hill and Cronenberg were signed on, King's involvement with the project was negligible.

With a keen eye on marquee appeal, Dino completed the major casting with Brooke Adams (*Altered States*) as Sarah, veteran British actor Herbert Lom as Dr. Sam Weizak and the versatile Martin Sheen as Greg Stillson. Actors from earlier Cronenberg pictures— *Scanners*, *The Brood* and *Videodrome*—also found parts. This family approach was continued in the casting of Ramon Estevez, Martin Sheen's son, as "the kid with the camera." When Johnny starts firing at him during a rally, Stillson's instincts get the better of him and he uses a small child as a human shield. Though both are unharmed, the Pulitzer-winning newsphoto of Stillson's politically uncool moves, snapped by "the kid with the camera," works better than any bullet in shooting down the politician's career.

Completed screenplay or no, Cronenberg was still open to improvising on the set. The most noticeable script departure arose out of an ad-lib by Christopher Walken, known for his offbeat sense of humor. While rehearsing the assassination scene, the actor joked that—oh, gosh—he couldn't shoot because the cowardly Stillson had grabbed none other than Sarah's child! Cronenberg thought this was a great idea. After all, Sarah and her husband were both volunteer workers for Stillson. The director held up filming until a child that fit the part could found and the scene reblocked.

Another example occurred during Johnny's vision of Stillson launching an nuclear attack on Russia. In the released film, Martin Sheen screams at a trepidatious general that if he doesn't place his palm on the scanning screen (used in firing the rockets), then he'll "hack it off and put it there for you!" This line was Sheen's improvisation, referring back to a discarded earlier draft of the script where Stillson actually shot the recalcitrant commander for his lack of cooperation.

As often happens, additional changes were made in the editing phase, some due to production problems, others from shifts in the director's concepts. A three minute prologue of Johnny's accident as a kid had been shot in order to set up his subsequent psychic powers. Cronenberg later dropped this sequence, deeming it a distraction from the overall story.

Physical problems were to blame for the re-editing of Johnny's first precognitive vision. After touching his nurse's arm, Johnny finds himself transported to her daughter's bedroom, now in flames. Originally, Walken was to be shown first in his hospital bed in the little girl's room, and then in the girl's bed as the flames dance around him. But problems with coordinating all the fire and physical effects limited the amount of usable footage. Cronenberg discovered that an E.T. doll could be clearly seen burning up in one of the shots, an unintended effect counterproductive to the scene. But it was too late to reshoot so only the elements with the child's bed made it into the final cut, sabotaging the director's extra touch of surrealism.

It was Cronenberg's original intention to place Johnny clearly within each visionary episode—seemingly part of the action yet helpless to affect it. After rethinking this concept he edited Walken out of all but two of such sequences: the bedroom fire and one of the Castle Rock rape-murders. (Careful viewers can briefly glimpse

Johnny's arm during the underwater shots of the hockey accident sequence. He had been filmed as drowning with the children.)

King's reaction to a rough cut of the picture initiated a further alteration of the climactic assassination sequence. In that version, Johnny momentarily hesitates when Stillson shields himself with Susan's baby, then fires anyway. King felt this showed Johnny was willing to sacrifice the child to get Stillson, a less than heroic attitude. Though Cronenberg felt a case could made for Johnny's actions—he was, after all, saving the planet from Stillson's nuclear madness—the director did agree that its effect was negative. The scene was recut, allowing Sarah to rescue her child before Johnny starts firing again.

King has voiced continuing reservations about the scene, however. ". . . It disturbs me that, of all the babies in New Hampshire, it turns out to be Sarah's own baby that Stillson happens to grab," he told a fan magazine. "A lot of plot choices reflect an obsession in Hollywood that everything has to support everything else, like a house of cards." This statement is quite true. Closure and rhyming are almost obsessively adhered to in commercial screenplays, regardless of story logic. It's interesting that this one instance was the result of a casual jest.

The Dead Zone opened very well, benefiting from the October season for thrillers that had recently been established with *Halloween* and its many imitators. (Traditionally, a fallow box office period existed from the end of summer to the Thanksgiving weekend.) Critics and fans alike responded to Cronenberg's restrained direction and the great performances he got from his cast, especially Walken. □

"Well, I did a screenplay for THE DEAD ZONE which was a Dino De Laurentiis production, and his feeling about that screenplay was that it was too involved, too convoluted. So they went back to Jeff— Jeffrey Boam, who had done a really dreadful first draft, and they all sat down and hammered out a pretty decent script."
—Speaking of *The Dead Zone* with Tim Hewett

DIRECTED BY JOHN CARPENTER

Bully boy Malcolm Danare keeps in shape with some nighttime jogging—paced by Christine.

CHRISTINE (1983)

Stephen King's 526-page tome, CHRISTINE, is a haunted car story. High school nerd Arnie Cunningham falls hard for a broken-down '58 Plymouth Fury, Christine. Love at first sight. But is the previous owner's evil spirit still racking up road time in the rusty hunk of Detroit iron? Or was this devil on wheels simply "born bad," consequently corrupting the souls of its owners while they rode behind the wheel? Arnie's best friend Dennis, his girlfriend Leigh, even his parents, all notice a change in the boy once Christine be-

Bad to the bone Christine and her siblings aborning on the Plymouth Fury assembly line.

CHRISTINE

A Columbia Pictures release, 12/83. 110 minutes (R). Directed by John Carpenter. Produced by Richard Kobritz. Screenplay by Bill Phillips. Co-Producer: Larry Franco. Associate Producer: Barry Bernardi. Executive Producers: Kirby McCauley & Mark Tarlov. Director of Photography: Donald M. Morgan. Editor: Marion Rothman. Original Music: John Carpenter, in association with Alan Howarth. Production Design: Daniel Lomino. Special Effects Supervisor: Roy Arbogast.

Arnie Cunningham . . . . .Keith Gordon
Dennis Guilder. . . . . .John Stockwell
Leigh Cabot. . . . . .Alexandra Paul
Will Darnell. . . . . .Robert Prosky
Rudolph Jenkins. . . . . .Harry Dean Stanton
Regina Cunningham . . . . .Christine Belford
George LeBay. . . . . .Roberts Blossom
Buddy Repperton . . . . .William Ostrander

Also: David Spielberg, Malcolm Danare, Steven Tash, Stuart Charns, Kelly Preston, Mark Poppel, Robert Darnell, Douglas Warhit, Bruce French, Keri Montgomery.

comes an inseparable part of his life. Will Dennis and Leigh be able to save their friend from his car? Bodywork ensues.

We first met Richard Kobritz as the producer of the *'Salem's Lot* miniseries back in 1979. In 1983 he would reteam with director John Carpenter to bring CHRISTINE to the movie theatres a mere 9 months after its hardcover publication in late 1982.

This supernaturally speedy transformation from big book to big screen began in the summer of 1982. Kirby McCauley, Stephen King's literary agent, sent Kobritz a pre-publication manuscript of CHRISTINE. Kobritz was still in the Warner Bros. television sector and now a senior president of production. He formed a partnership with Mark Tarlov of Polar Films, they made a bid on the property— and got it. Kobritz began thinking seriously about quitting his job of eight years.

Kobritz's first choice for director was John Carpenter, who at that time had directed such features as *The Fog, Escape From New York* and *The Thing* (and more recently *Starman* and *Big Trouble in Little China*). Carpenter was already familiar with CHRISTINE and he didn't take long to agree with Kobritz that they should make the picture together. Interestingly, the director had recently terminated his involvement with another King film, *Firestarter*, over at Universal. Another past-participant with *Firestarter* was screenwriter Bill Phillips. The young writer's final (and uncredited) rewrite on that project favorably impressed Kobritz and he signed on Phillips to adapt CHRISTINE.

"With friends like these who needs an Inquisition?" wonders beleaguered Arnie (Keith Gordon).

Every writer's fiction presents a particular challenge or problem when it is to be translated to the screen. Kobritz has said he does not feel the sheer length of King's books is the special problem when trying to adapt his works, but rather, the difficulty is in finding a viable way to translate King's central generating horror literary device—namely, all those creepy interior monologues. When adapting CHRISTINE, much of the novel's elements were streamlined by eliminating or compositing extraneous characters and likewise condensing the action. The central characters and events were left relatively untouched. In fact, much of the dialogue was taken directly from King's text.

The screenplay also resolved the origin of Christine's evil nature. King admits to hedging his bets on just how the demonic car got to be so bad. Possibly the car was just "born bad," gradually possessing its owner, Roland LeBay, until he self-destructed. Or, after a time, Christine became a rolling haven for Roland LeBay's demonic spirit, with the impressionable Arnie Cunningham just the first hapless victim to happen by. The filmmaker's opted for the former explanation. An opening flashback sequence of Christine's Detroit birth was created to show unmistakably that, as George Thorogood's rocking soundtrack accompaniment explains, this is a mean machine born "bad to the bone."

The rest of King's story rocks along steady and unstoppable, or as King has characterized it, "an outrageous kind of riff on one chord." Arnie begins restoring the decrepit car and we see his own

Would you buy a used car from this man? LeBay (Roberts Blossom) in Christine.

Hell hath no Fury like Christine scorned. Arnie's pals will soon receive a nasty lesson in bodywork.

character deteriorate while his "nerdiness" transmutes into a kind of "greaser" cool. His family helplessly watches Arnie turn into a "mean machine" himself and Dennis and Leigh begin recognizing Christine for the supernatural menace she is, especially after some mysterious hit and run accidents occur around town. (It's amazing how similar this plot is to *Little Shop of Horrors*.)

Keith Gordon (*Dressed to Kill*) did a great job with Arnie's gradual Jekyll and Hyde character transformation. Arnie's two closest friends, and near-victims, Dennis and Leigh, were portrayed by John Stockwell and Alexandra Paul. Character actors Roberts Blossom, Harry Dean Stanton (*Escape from New York*) and Robert Prosky rounded out the major adult parts.

Budgeted at $10 million, big name stars were purposely eschewed in order to both give more weight to the film's real star, Christine; and to put more production value on the screen, since the final script called for numerous (and expensive) stunts and floor effects. Another budgetary consideration prompted moving the book's location from Pittsburgh to Southern California (though Carpenter insisted that no palm trees be visible in the scenes).

Before production could begin in April 1983, Kobritz (who had by then quit his job at Warner) had to search the United States and Canada for '58 Plymouth Furys. After advertising in newspapers across the country, he eventually spent $500,000 to round up twenty-three of the vehicles. In various states of repair, the vehicles were reassembled into seventeen identical Christine picture cars (two survived the filming in mint condition).

It fell to special effects artist Roy Arbogast to not only destroy Christine in a variety of creative ways but also to stage the car's miraculous self-repairs "live" on camera. While some of these effects could be achieved through cutaways and reverse filming, Arbogast also constructed several live-action props that would undent, untwist and unmangle themselves on cue. These included grills, fenders, hoods and, at one point, an entire front end.

Like King's book, the music of classic rock 'n' roll both punctuated and commented on the story. "I grew up in the Fifties," the writer said. "For me, rock 'n' roll was the rise of consciousness. . . . That's when I really started to live, and that was brought on by the music of the Fifties." Aside from the picture's plethora of hot tunes (the soundtrack album is a great party record), director John Carpenter (himself an accomplished musician) fashioned the film's non-Top 40 musical themes. (Beginning with his first feature, *Dark Star*, in 1974, Carpenter has created original music for most of his films and has several soundtrack albums in print. Charlie Chaplin was another major director who wrote scores for his pictures.)

Like most horror films, *Christine* enjoyed a peppy opening weekend. But despite everyone's proficient efforts it soon ran out of box office gas, proving to be a disappointment to Columbia Pictures.

" 'The Shining' was open right until the end. I didn't know what was going to happen until the very end. That shows in the book. The original plan was for them all to die up there and for Danny to become the controlling force of the hotel after he died. And the psychic force of the hotel would go up exponentially. . . . But I got connected with the kid. In the first draft of the book Jack beats his wife to death with the mallet and it was blood and brains and everything. It was really just terrible and I couldn't do it. I couldn't leave it that way."

—Speaking of *The Shining* with Marty Ketchum, et al.

"I'll be *back*."

CHILDREN OF THE CORN

DIRECTED BY FRITZ KIERSCH

John Franklin plays the demonic boy cult leader Isaac in Children of the Corn.

CHILDREN OF THE CORN (1984)

Normally, short stories are not bestselling, high-profile literary properties of the kind that producers rush to acquire and studios jump to finance. But if your name happens to be Stephen King, well . . .

King has stated that he believes the short story form to be more difficult to master than novels, a view that many novelists agree with. Short story writing has to be much more concise, the themes and concepts more tightly focused. King's first sales were short stories and he makes it a point to create a few shorter tales every year, even though his novels sell for multi-millions. King feels that

Hope I die before I grow old: Aging corn cultists strip down in preparation for ritual suicide.

CHILDREN OF THE CORN

A New World Pictures release (Angles Entertainment Group, Inverness Prod., Hal Roach Studios, Cinema Group Ventures), 6/84. 93 minutes (R). Directed by Fritz Kiersch. Produced by Donald P. Borchers & Terrence Kirby. Screenplay by George Goldsmith. Executive Producer: Earl Glick & Charles K. Webber. Associate Producer: Mark Lipson. Director of Photography: Raoul Lomas. Editor: Harry Keramidas. Original Music: Johnathan Elias. Art Director: Craig Stearns. Production Supervisor: Michael Winter. Special Visual Effects: Max A. Anderson. Special Effects: SPFX. Inc. & Eric Rumsey.

Burt Stanton . . . . .Peter Horton
Vicky Baxter . . . . .Linda Hamilton
Diehl . . . . .R.G. Armstrong
Isaac . . . . .John Franklin
Malachai . . . . .Courtney Gains
Job . . . . .Robby Kiger
Sarah . . . . .Annemarie McEvoy
Rachel. . . . . .Julie Maddalena
Joseph. . . . . .Jonas Marlowe

Also: Dan Snook, David Cowen, Suzy Southam, D.G. Johnson, Patrick Boylan, Elmer Soderstrom, Teresa Coigo, Mitch Carter.

the skill it takes to write good short fiction is like a muscle, and it will atrophy if not exercised regularly.

King's first short story collection, NIGHT SHIFT (1978), provided him with a treasure trove of raw material for theatrical adaptation. Following *'Salem's Lot*, NBC television wasted King's time with an abortive *Night Shift* series, which would have had the author hosting each week, in the manner of Rod Serling's *Night Gallery*. English producer Milton Subotsky, a longtime figure on the British horror scene, optioned six stories for two proposed trilogies. King himself, still learning the screenplay trade, wrote treatments and scripts using some of the NIGHT SHIFT material.

One of these adapted stories was "Children of the Corn." In this gruesome tale, Burt and Vicky, an innocent couple on their honeymoon, stray from the major highways during a cross-country trip through Nebraska's corn country. Suddenly a young boy pops out of nowhere and gets himself run over. Seeking help in the nearby village of Gatlin, the couple finds the place eerily deserted, and with corn strung up everywhere. Before you can say "Lord of the Flies," they're menaced by a cult of murderous kids who took over the town thirteen years ago by massacring all the adults. With no member older than nineteen, the pack appears to be getting commands from some kind of demonic (and hungry) deity, the unseen "He Who Walks Behind the Rows" which lurks in the surrounding cornfields. Corn-age ensues.

Children of the Corn followed a tortuous path to production. King claims to have lost track of how many times the property has been sold and re-sold. It appears that initial interest in King's screenplay came from Varied Directions, a small production company hoping to make the picture for $1 million with David Hoffman directing. Hopes were not enough. In early 1979 Harry Wiland, a 34-year-old documentary-filmmaker from Rockport, Maine, called up Stephen King (living in Bangor) and asked if they could do a project together. "I've always wanted to do a relatively low-budget feature film," Wiland told a reporter at the time. "If you know what you're doing you can get a great deal of production value on the screen for a lot less money."

Let us reflect on the phrase, "if you know what you're doing."

According to King, Wiland and his partner, producer Joseph Masefield, submitted several original scripts to him, none of which he liked. He sent them *Children of the Corn*, and a low-money deal was eventually worked out, for better or worse.

"For years, I've desperately wanted to get film crews into Maine," King told a journalist. "There are parts of Washington County where 12 weeks of shooting could generate more income than the place sees in a year. Wiland came along with production facilities on call and got the rights for a song—as Laurel [George Romero] did for *Creepshow* and THE STAND."

Wiland and King worked on two additional drafts of the screenplay. At the filmmakers' request a Vietnam war subtext was injected. The groom became a Viet vet and it was noted that the children took over Gatlin in the politically restless year of 1968. How the clan of killer kids could become a metaphor for Viet Cong jungle fighters still remains a mystery.

At this point, a partnership between Home Box Office and 20th Century-Fox was on-line to bankroll the production's $2.75 million budget, with Lance Kerwin, the kid from 'Salem's Lot, starring. But Fox backed out right before the start of shooting, which left Wiland and Masefield with no production funds and a rapidly dissolving partnership.

One of the terms of this dissolution was that each had one year to get the project off the ground. Neither man accomplished it, though Canada's Filmplan and then United Artists both took nibbles. Eventually Hal Roach Studios picked up the project and commissioned George Goldsmith to do a rewrite (which we now know is the first thing a new production house does after picking up a prop-

---

"And then, the second, very moral question is: do you have any right, just because you're a big shot, to steal screen credit from somebody who's an unknown. What if it's a great film? So, I thought about that one very very hard for about three days, and then I decided essentially, I couldn't trust New World Pictures. I sent a telegram to the screenwriter's guild and said that I didn't want to respond to Clayton's [Goldsmith's] petition to have sole screen credit on the picture, so he was granted sole screen credit. I'm delighted that he was on both counts. Number one, the picture was a dog; it was a shuck-and-jive situation. What they had sent me and represented as the final screenplay had nothing in common at all with what finally made it to the screen. It was basically, I think, an effort into accepting a screen credit that didn't belong to me."
—Speaking of *Children of the Corn* with Tim Hewitt

Not even the auto club can lend a hand when the Children of the Corn stalk their victim's cars.

erty). Goldsmith considered the King script not up to its potential. "It's dreamlike, which is characteristic of King's work," Goldsmith commented at the time. "I wanted to make clearer, more linear, certain ideas he touched upon but did not develop."

One of Goldsmith's additions was to create four major supporting players as part of the band of kids: a young brother and sister, Job and Sarah, who are disaffected with the group; and two older members, Isaac and Malachai, who run the cult and eventually fight each other for its control. The ending was also made more upbeat, allowing Burt and Vicky to destroy "The Walker" and get any kids still living back on the right track. Goldsmith felt that proper expression of his ideas on the nature of cultism and the dangers of blind adherence to faith and dogma "precluded the defeat of my protagonists." He also recognized the fact that killing off the film's two leads probably wouldn't help at the box office.

By 1983, a version of Goldsmith's draft reached Donald Borchers, a senior VP at New World Pictures, a reliable Hollywood film factory known for making or releasing a high volume of discount-budget genre pictures. Seeing gold in a relatively unattached King property, especially if they could beat out the higher-priced King films then currently in production (*Firestarter* and *Cat's Eye*),

New World jumped into bed with the Roach Studios and the production swiftly got into high gear.

First-time feature director Fritz Kiersch helmed the project. Terrence Kirby, his partner in a commercial filmmaking company, co-produced the film with Borchers. In only one month, the $3 million picture was rushed into a 27-day shoot in order to make use of the soon-to-be harvested cornfields—surely some kind of record.

"I hope the film is controversial, enlightening and intelligent," Goldsmith said before its release. "There are going to be people who will understand the underlying metaphors and ideas, and people who won't. They'll both come out of the theatre satisfied."

One has to wonder about the screenwriter's ideas. Though totally unseen in the original story, the "walker behind the rows" is an actual entity, out there in the fields demanding blood sacrifices and unquestioning obedience. The being may be an evil creature, a bit of drag to live with, but it's not just a product of some bizarre religion's blind faith—the thing is *real*, the kids witness its power. How this was transmuted by the scripter's professed intention to imbue the work with a cinematic subtext of imperialistic adventurism and social Darwinism not many would care to find out.

The question of screen credit again came up before the picture's release. Already the picture was being billed as "Stephen King's *Children of the Corn*." New World Pictures was, in King's words, "hot to have *my name* on the screenplay!" The studio sent a copy of the script to the Writers Guild with King's name on it, applying for sole screen credit for the novelist. Goldsmith protested, and King was asked to respond.

King recalled the situation for an interviewer. "Now the copy of the screenplay I saw for *Children of the Corn*, supposedly the final

---

"The comic, that was my idea. They wanted a novelization, they wanted to farm it out, and I told them I've never allowed anything to be novelized and I said that if we're going to do this then let's do it in the spirit of the movie itself, which is of the EC comics, the horror pulps, let's go ahead and do a comic book.

"So we hired a guy called Berni Wrightson to do the panels and I just did the continuity. It was kinda fun."
—Speaking of *Creepshow* with Edwin Pouncey

---

screenplay, had large portions of *my* screenplay that I had written four or five years ago. I even recognized the typescript from the Olivetti that I used at the time." After much agonizing contemplation, King finally decided that he simply couldn't trust New World about the script, and that just because he was a bestselling writer, taking credit for another writer's effort wasn't cool. King refused to challenge the protest and Goldsmith's petition for sole screen credit was granted.

King had no reason to regret his decision, later calling the picture "a dog; it was a shuck and jive situation. What they had sent me and represented as the final screenplay had nothing in common at all with what finally made it to the screen."

New World did get the jump on its King-film competitors and with a negative cost of only $3 million (the direct cost of production), and another $4 million to open the picture, they soon recouped their expenses, and made money on the video rights and foreign revenues.

The response to *Children of the Corn*, a clumsy string of cliched horror film situations, was universally negative. "Some of the worst performances by children in recent memory are the featured attraction of this limp melodrama," concluded reviewer David Ehrenstien in a trade publication.

Illogical in the extreme, the film did boast a bloody opening sequence of the children taking over Gatlin. In the story, thirteen years pass before Burt and Vicky stumble into town. This was shortened to three years in the film, but should have been three months since none of the kids seem to have aged or even changed their clothes. The depiction of the "walker" was, as in the story, left largely to the viewers' imagination. But the filmmakers had to show *something*, so the rows of corn were made to part mysteriously and the ground roiled most menacingly. This effect was achieved by putting a fire hose under a dirt carpet and pumping air through it. We all know how scary moving lumps of earth can be. A simple optical double printing shows a demonic presence in the flames of the burning cornfield for the climactic final scene.

The film was shot near Sioux City, Iowa using a non-union crew. Television's Linda Hamilton, hungry for work at that time, starred as Vicky. She would go on to other things in *The Terminator, Black Moon Rising* and *King Kong Lives*. □

FIRE-STARTER

DIRECTED BY MARK L. LESTER

Department of Scientific Intelligence babysitter John Rainbird (George C. Scott) cradles Drew Barrymore in Firestarter.

FIRESTARTER (1984)

Classified by Stephen King as essentially a science fiction tale, FIRESTARTER tells the story of 8-year-old Charlene "Charlie" McGee. Her parents, Andrew and Vicky, are two one-time subjects of secret drug tests conducted in the Sixties by "The Shop," a top secret government weapons lab. The McGees' unusual daughter has a talent for mentally starting fires through controlled pyrokinesis. Having monitored this family (since the Sixties) The Shop now wants to harness Charlie's combustive talents. Very, very badly. Agents from The Shop murder Vicky and go after Charlie and Andy as if they were Libyan terrorists. Andy McGee possesses a few cranial tricks of his

Young Charlie shows her budget-minded parents (David Keith and Heather Locklear) how to avoid the expense of a new microwave.

FIRESTARTER

A Universal Pictures release (Dino De Laurentiis), 10/84. 115 minutes (R). Directed by Mark L. Lester. Produced by Frank Capra, Jr. Screenplay by Stanley Mann. Associate Producer: Martha Schumacher. Director of Photography: Guiseppe Ruzzolini. Editor: David Rawlins. Original Music: Tangerine Dream. Art Director: Giorgio Postiglione. Make-up Effects: Jose Sanchez. Special Effects: Mike Wood & Jeff Jarvis. Stunt Coordinator: Glenn Randall.

Andy McGee . . . . David Keith
Charlie McGee . . . . Drew Barrymore
Captain Hollister . . . . Martin Sheen
John Rainbird . . . . George C. Scott
Irv Manders . . . . Art Carney
Norma Manders . . . . Louise Fletcher
Dr. Joseph Wanless . . . . Freddie Jones
Vicky McGee . . . . Heather Locklear
Dr. Pynchot . . . . Moses Gunn

Also: Antonio Vargas, Orville Jamieson, Curtis Credel, Keith Colbert, Richard Warlock, Jeff Ramey, Jack Manger, Lisa Ann Barnes, Larry Sprinkle, Cassandra Ward-Freeman, Scott R. Davis, Nina Jones, William Alspaugh, Laurens Moore, Anne Fitzgibbon, Steve Boles, Stanley Mann, Robert Miano, Leon Rippy.

own, though using them, like Johnny Smith in THE DEAD ZONE, is damaging to his health. Mental mayhem ensues.

King reports that his research for FIRESTARTER turned up many well-documented, and mystifying, cases of pyrokinesis. With this phenomenon, spontaneous combustion occurs from within, burning the victim beyond recognition, even to complete ash—yet leaving beds or furniture virtually untouched. If you've read PSY-CHIC DISCOVERIES BEHIND THE IRON CURTAIN, you'll know that these incidents have apparently been recorded all over the world.

The story of novel-into-film starts back in 1981, before the book's publication. According to King, FIRESTARTER's film rights were initially purchased for $1 million by Dodi Fayed, an Egyptian film producer planning to make the picture through Allied Stars, an English production house. Fayed's plans apparently went up in smoke for the project next surfaces at Universal Studios under the auspices of executive producer Dino De Laurentiis. There, director

Caution, evil geniuses at work: John Rainbird (George C. Scott) and Capt. Hollister (Martin Sheen) compare resumes.

John Carpenter supervised script rewrites by Bill Phillips. Phillips was working from a previous set of drafts that Bill Lancaster had written for De Laurentiis. At this point, the *Firestarter* screenplay had removed the pivotal character of John Rainbird, The Shop's psychotic assassin, in favor of an evil lady doctor. Also called for were lots of expensive special effects and fire stunts.

Once burned and twice shy after Carpenter's expensive and effects laden (and deliciously gross) remake of *The Thing* rolled over like a sick dog at the box office, Universal terminated preproduction work on *Firestarter*. The Carpenter/Phillips team would go on to work with Richard Kobritz on CHRISTINE while De Laurentiis commissioned yet another screenplay. Undaunted, the producer turned to seasoned pro Stanley Mann for a new set of drafts. Mann is well known in the industry for a variety of projects (including *The Collector, Omen II, Conan II* [for De Laurentiis], *Meteor*, and *The Eye of the Needle*).

Stanley Mann's efforts were more to Universal's liking. The screenwriter toned down the picture's expensive effects and didn't stray so much from King's novel. Placated, Universal once again "green-lighted" the project, which was now budgeted at $15 million. Next, De Laurentiis signed on director Mark L. Lester. Lester had originally worked as a documentary filmmaker before toiling in the

Charlie and her dad (David Keith) seek refuge at the Manders (Art Carney and Louise Fletcher) farm.

Was it something I said? DSI agents think twice about attempting to capture runaway Charlie McGee.

low-budget field with efforts such as *Truck Stop Women, Gold of the Amazon Women, Roller Boogie*. These movies all demonstrated a good eye for action and a casual sense of humor. His latest feature, *The Class of '84*, had caught the attention of De Laurentiis.

The production now relocated to North Carolina. De Laurentiis was at that time replanting his European film empire in America's rich soil. He had mothballed his studios in Rome and begun constructing temporary soundstages in the economically attractive area of Wilmington, North Carolina. (Unlike California, North Carolina is a "right-to-work" state, free from the unions and guilds that control the film craftsmen which make up the "below the line" production costs. Reducing manufacturing costs is one effective method for controlling rising budgets, but some would contend that union labor is cheap compared to the multi-millions producers pay up front to film stars in order to get their pictures funded.)

While the screenplay still called for a fair amount of pyrotechnical effects, De Laurentiis decided to strengthen his production package by employing the reliable "a cast of stars" disaster-film formula, as typified in *The Towering Inferno* and *Meteor*. A host of familiar faces were hired to bring *Firestarter* to life: George C. Scott as the villainous Rainbird. Martin Sheen as the amoral Shop leader (in his second King feature, filling in after scheduling problems forced Burt Lancaster to bow out). David Keith (*The Right Stuff*) as Andy McGee with Heather Locklear (*Dynasty*) his doomed wife, Vicky. Art Carney and Louise Fletcher as the sympathetic Middle Americans. And finally, that adorable cutie from *E.T.*, seven-year-old Drew Barrymore as Charlie McGee. A good smattering of lesser known names, like Moses Gunn and Freddie Jones, filled out the cast. And sure enough, the picture turned out to be a total disaster.

The hefty budget, imposing cast, and the many potentially dangerous stunts were a lot for Mark Lester to handle on this, his first real "Hollywood" feature. Lester stated at the time that he initially felt some intimidation with the big league project, but thanks to the cast's support, De Laurentiis's enthusiastic involvement, and his own confidence in the script, these feelings of trepidation soon disappeared.

Mann's script also impressed King, who called it the best adaptation of his work to that date. Though not directly involved with this production, the writer would soon be working with Dino and Drew.

The production shooting schedule lasted 67 days in and around

---

"Dino was very taken with the concept of the little girl and the cat, and he thought that the cat would make a wonderful device to bind the three stories together. He said, 'Stephen, can you put the cat in all three stories? Do you see a way that that could be done?' And I thought to myself, c'mon, the guy's got to be crazy. It's impossible. But I went back and I thought about it and I actually saw a way that it could be done. I got very excited about it and I called him up: 'Dino! Dino! I know how you can do this!' He says: 'Ees wonderfol. Now, what about de gorl?' and I said, 'Dino, do you know what you're asking?' But I saw a way that that could be done as well. Then, I thought the concept was so unusual and so spacey that I wanted to write it myself. I thought that he might offer me the chance to do the whole screenplay, and when he did I jumped at it."
—Speaking of *Cat's Eye* with Tim Hewitt

Drew Barrymore listens attentively but still has trouble figuring out how Scott ever managed to win an Oscar.

the Wilmington area. A lovingly preserved Southern mansion dou-bled as The Shop's deceptively-genteel headquarters. Knowing how to stretch a dollar, De Laurentiis decided to make his temporary studios permanent. He has since established Wilmington as one of the busiest domestic film producing centers outside of Hollywood.

The fire effects did prove quite spectacular. Many of the stunts had never been attempted on such a large scale before. The judicious use of dummies, radio-controlled squibs, hidden gas jets, catapults, air cannons, trained stunt doubles and camera angles helped pull off the live effects without a single injury or incident. (The specter of the then-recent *Twilight Zone* fatal accident was looming large on everyone's mind.) The scope of the stunts had been aided by new innovations in flame-retardant gels, clothing materials and light-weight breathing apparatuses. As many as ten cameras were used to catch these "one time only" stunts.

A quarter of a million dollars in lumber was used in duplicating the film's plantation setting, so it could be burned down during the final confrontation. Charlie McGee's climactic display of pyrokinetic dexterity was in part accomplished using ten-inch styrofoam balls coated with rubber cement which were then sent flaming along fine metal wires powered by model rocket engines.

Since the skeletons available from India (the world's skeleton headquarters) were too small, polyester skulls and skeletons were constructed for use in melting the baddies on screen. In certain cases, full-sized, rod-animated puppets were employed when frying specific personalities on screen. (Real skulls couldn't accommodate the special make-up—usually sculptured in gelatin or alginite from life-masks—used to recreate the doomed characters.)

For all this effort and castability, the American filmgoing public just did not respond to *Firestarter*. More like a bloated, out-of-control miniseries than top-flight theatrical entertainment, the picture quickly fizzled at the box office. Referring to the infamous 1970 filming of Gore Vidal's controversial pop novel (one of the most celebrated "bombs" ever made), King remarked, "*Firestarter* could have been *Myra Breckinridge* with a push in just the other direction, if there would've been just something else a little bit grotesque added to it."

But De Laurentiis's confidence in Lester was not misplaced. The director went on to make the popular Arnold Schwarzenegger action-picture for DEG, *Commando*. □

"Well, they are hilarious. I saw part of the 'Quitters, Inc.' story, and I laughed harder than I've laughed at anything that I've seen in the theatres this year, with the exception of one serious picture, which I thought was pretty funny—STAR TREK III, I just laughed and laughed. I couldn't stop. 'Course I have a different reference. My brother went bald at eighteen, got Jesus at twenty-three, got Amway at thirty, and now he wears this wig and looks just like a sort of gone-to-seed William Shatner. I made that connection and just started to laugh."

—Speaking of *Cat's Eye* with Tim Hewitt

Cat's Eye

DIRECTED BY LEWIS TEAGUE

Who let the cat in? Drew Barrymore, James Naughton and Candy Clark in Cat's Eye.

CAT'S EYE (1984)

Italian film producer Dino De Laurentiis is truly one of the last independents whose personal style and business manners reflect the great Hollywood moguls of the Thirties and Forties. Unafraid of artistic and financial risks—or of shamelessly hyping his product— De Laurentiis combines showmanship, business acumen and artistic merit in his annual slate of pictures. Long a power in Europe, and with strong Hollywood connections, De Laurentiis mothballed his Rome studios in the mid-Seventies and moved operations to Amer-

James Woods quits smoking the hard way with help from Alan King (left) and Tony Munafo.

CAT'S EYE

A MGM/United Artists release, 8/84. 94 minutes (PG-13). Directed by Lewis Teague. Produced by Martha Schumacher. Original Screenplay by Stephen King. Executive Producer: Dino De Laurentiis. Co-Producer: Milton Subotsky. Director of Photography: Jack Cardiff. Editor: Scott Conrad. Original Music: Adam Silvestri. Production Executive: John M. Eckert. Production Design: Giorgio Postiglione. Creatures Creator: Carlo Rimbaldi. Special Effects Coordinator: Jeff Jarvis. Special Visual Effects: Barry Nolan.

Amanda/Our Girl . . . . .Drew Barrymore
Morrison . . . . .James Woods
Dr. Donati . . . . .Alan King
Cressner . . . . .Kenneth McMillan
Norris . . . . .Robert Hays
Sally Ann. . . . . .Candy Clark
Hugh. . . . . .James Naughton
Junk. . . . . .Tony Munafo

Also: Court Miller, Russell Horton, Patricia Benson, Mary D'Arcy, James Rebhorn, Jack Dillon, Susan Hawes, Shelley Burch, Sal Richards, Jesse Doran, Patricia Kalember, Mike Starr, Charles Dutton.

ica. At first he functioned largely as an executive producer who made a series of distribution deals with the major studios. (*Dead Zone* was released by Paramount, *Firestarter* through Universal.) But this was just a stepping stone to larger things.

De Laurentiis values his relationships and believes in the people he works with, which surely accounts for much of his success. One such relationship is with Stephen King, who has said, "Dino is the sort of guy who would take a chance on Jack the Ripper if he thought he could get a good picture out of him." Adding that "he's treated me with a lot of dignity and respect. I respect him. That's why I've done more business with him than anybody else." At last count, this has resulted in six different productions.

So even before the ill-fated *Firestarter* was released, De Laurentiis and staff producer Martha J. Schumacher struck a deal with King for an anthology-style screenplay. The major source material for this project? Why, those often-optioned short stories from King's NIGHT SHIFT collection. De Laurentiis and Schumacher had the relative luxury of being able to choose from seven of the NIGHT SHIFT tales. They had gathered the necessary rights from UK producer Milton Subotsky and (according to King) The Production Company. This California production company had tried to get a *Night Shift* TV-movie off the ground after NBC's attempted development of a *Night Shift* series in the wake of the *'Salem's Lot* miniseries.

"So Dino had some stories and he had some ideas about doing a film that would interrelate the stories," King later told a magazine reporter. "He was very taken with Drew Barrymore, and he asked could I write an original." King was visiting the De Laurentiis *Firestarter* set in Wilmington, NC at the time, and, as the writer recalled, "I had had an idea for a story for some time. It dealt with a little boy who was saved from a monster that lived in his wall by his pet cat, and the cat would have a bad rep because the mother would think that cats can steal your breath and all that stuff." 24 hours later King had written the idea as a short little screenplay. "After changing the sex from boy to girl, the part fit Drew perfectly."

According to King, De Laurentiis was "very taken with the concept of the little girl and the cat, and he thought that the cat would make a wonderful device to bind the three stories together." As King tells it, he thought De Laurentiis was crazy when he asked the writer to find a means of using the cat as a linking device. The two NIGHT SHIFT stories selected were "The Ledge," about an adulterous tennis pro being terrorized by his lover's gangster/gambler husband, and "Quitters, Inc.," concerning a self-help company's strong-arm methods for persuading their clients to kick smoking and lose weight. Never one to shrink from a challenge, King managed to concoct a feline connector for the trio of tales.

Pleased, De Laurentiis then asked King if he could find a way to link the girl into the stories as well. (Beginning to see how this guy operates?) "I said, 'Dino, do you know what you're asking?' But I saw a way that that could be done as well. Then, I thought the concept was so unusual and spacey that I wanted to write it myself." De Laurentiis offered King the chance to do the screenplay and the writer immediately accepted. The resulting project, *Cat's Eye*, would be the first full-screenplay involvement for King since *Creepshow*, four years previous (which Dino reportedly had never seen).

At King's suggestion, a script was sent to Lewis Teague, the director of another King creature feature, *Cujo*. (Teague's most recent film is *The Jewel of the Nile*, the sequel to *Romancing the Stone*.) The director responded to the screenplay's light tone and black humor. He saw it as a good change of pace from the horrific rigors of his earlier rabid dog romp. With plenty of time for preproduction planning (unusual in the "hurry up and wait" film world), Teague and King were able to revise the script to their mutual satisfaction. King felt that the feline linking device, which effectively made the cat the picture's "star," helped the picture play more as a continuous feature, not merely as vignettes strung together. Teague concurred, believing that the flaws of a picture like *Twilight Zone— The Movie*, which required its audience to accommodate a completely new set of characters, situations and directorial styles every twenty minutes, were avoided by having the same writer, director and diagesic universe.

King has said that he was so happy with the material in his first draft that he decided not to include what he calls his "divorce clause" in his contract. This agreement allows King the right to simply walk away from a project if the director or producer demands too many changes in his work (like suddenly having the action set in outer space). This arrangement is a neat reversal on the standard "step deal" between producer and writer, which establishes a series of "cut-offs" where the producer retains the right to terminate their deal after each set of drafts or rewrites.

"But I loved what I had," King has stated, discussing the script,

*Who needs elevators? Betting man Robert Hays likes his view of the skyline
unobstructed by nuisances like windows and balconies.*

"and frankly, I didn't want anyone else to screw around with it."

Cat's Eye was to feature De Laurentiis's newest starlet, Drew
Barrymore. De Laurentiis wanted this King-spawned picture to
really be different, namely rated PG-13 instead of R. Then recently
introduced, the PG-13 rating (brought about by films like *Gremlins*
and *Indiana Jones and the Temple of Doom*) would theoretically
address a previously untapped audience (young teens) while still
having enough "bite" to satisfy King's fans. Budgeted between $5
and $7 million, the picture was the first feature to be made entirely at
the Italian producer's American production facilities in Wilmington,
NC (which De Laurentiis had established after shooting *Firestarter*
there).

References to King's literary milieu abound in the film. "Walk-
ons" by Christine and Cujo appear in the first few minutes and
characters are seen reading King novels or watching King films on
television while asking, "Who writes this crap, anyway?" Starring in
the first segment, "Quitters, Inc.," were James Woods (*Videodrome*)
as the harried smoker, and comedian Alan King as the jovially sadis-
tic no-smoking disciplinarian. "The Ledge" segment featured Robert
Hays (*Airplane*) as the philandering tennis pro, and Kenneth McMillan (*Dune*) as the cuckolded Cressner. And "The General" sequence

(named after Drew's on-screen kitty) featured Ms. Barrymore, Candy Clark (*Blue Thunder*) as her anti-feline mom, and James Naughton as her dad.

Though not demanding *Star Wars*-styled special effects, King's screenplay did necessitate a large amount of "special" staging, including complicated performances from the picture's nominal feline star. Animal trainer Karl Miller (from *Cujo*) "auditioned" thirty-five "tiger" cats for the title role, and sixteen responded well enough to training to appear in the film. Three cats, however, ultimately did the bulk of the work. Unlike their canine colleagues, feline thespians respond only to the "food reward" training method. For cats, the need to please humans has a rather low priority, so for them it's "if we don't eat, we don't work." The major problem with this is that their tiny little kitty stomachs soon fill up with munchies, which limits the possibility of using bribes of food. Most stunts or sequences have to be broken down for animal actors, much like choreography, into simple actions which are performed by different (and not too-full) specialty-cats (i.e.: one that jumps out of windows, one that curls up on beds, one that does nude scenes, etc.).

The "Quitters, Inc." segment called for construction of some special props and animated puppets for James Woods's on-screen hallucinations from nicotine withdrawal. Giant cigarettes menaced him. A plate of fried eggs with eyes for yolks watched his torment.

"The Ledge" required extensive use of forced perspective miniatures and elevated sets in order to make Robert Hays's reluctant walk around the 6-inch cornice of a luxury penthouse appear to be atop an Atlantic City hotel. The three-dimensional views of the hotel and surrounding cityscape were constructed by Emilio Ruiz, who prefers to work alone and rarely explains to his assistants how he does what he does. His unique miniatures are made to photographed from just one angle and look weird and out of proportion when viewed normally. But through the camera the illusion a great depth and vast distance is achieved. Ruiz rejects geometry in favor of "eyeballing" the handcrafting of his models, using an unmounted wide-angle lens to check his work. Other views of the city's nighttime skyline were accomplished with large, back-lit photographic transparencies. Model cars mounted on conveyor belts added to the general feeling of agrophobia.

The most elaborate production efforts were expended on the concluding "General" sequence where the cat must successfully bat-

The walls are alive with a pint-sized, dagger-wielding menace in Drew Barry-more's overstuffed bedroom.

tle a little but lethal troll in order to save Drew's life. De Laurentiis wanted to stay away from optical effects and stop-motion puppets. He called upon longtime associate and master creature-builder, Carlo Rimbaldi (*E.T.*, *Close Encounters*), to construct the elaborate and uncannily expressive troll-head for use in live-action filming on huge "oversize" sets.

Without resorting to any electronic servo-motors or similar de-vices, Rimbaldi's construction featured twenty-five different points of movement, all controlled by twelve levers attached to cables run-ning into the back of the puppet's head. The head itself could be worn by an actor when full-body shots were required. A complex arrangement of spring-loaded actuators and gimbal devices permit-ted the troll a wide range of convincing expressions. In other shots, a "real-size" hand puppet was used (the troll was supposed to be only inches tall), often manipulated by the director when working with

Barrymore. A simple lightweight mask was employed when the action got particularly acrobatic.

As with such classic science fiction films like *Dr. Cyclops* and *The Incredible Shrinking Man*, huge props duplicating the little girl's bedroom were used for staging the bulk of the troll's antics. In fact, the production entered THE GUINNESS BOOK OF WORLD RECORDS for constructing the world's largest set of bed and pillows. Similar to the gigantic gorilla hand used in *King Kong* (which De Laurentiis successfully remade in 1976), giant cat-paws attacked the troll when the action couldn't be cheated by cutaways and inserts. Thanks to judicious planning and skillful editing, the footage between the normal and oversize bedroom sets, punctuated by close-ups of the real cats and the puppet troll-head, created a rather exciting showdown.

Opening in April of '84, the picture did not do well with either critics or audiences. In fact it bombed, grossing around $8 million (which, when the cost of prints and ads are included, would have it losing at least $5 million domestically). One reason may have been that half of King's linking devices were removed from the finished film, dropped apparently at the behest of Frank Yablans, then president of the picture's releasing company.

It seems that in King's version the picture opened with a child's funeral and with the girl's distraught mother blaming the family cat for sucking out the kid's breath. The persecuted pet narrowly eludes the crazed woman, who goes after it with her husband's submachine gun! After the cat escapes, the ghost of the little girl (Drew) implores the cat to find her real killer, which apparently is some kind of evil little creature holed up in the wall of her bedroom.

So off the kitty goes, compelled by intermittent visions of the girl ("Our Girl" in the credits but also referred to as Amanda), taking us on a "cat's eye" view through the three stories. Starting the picture with the aftermath of a child's murder and then grave violence against a defenseless pet didn't sit right with the studio, since the picture was being billed as light entertainment, so out went the beginning. Another reason for the film's commercial failure could possibly have been the absence of a planned cameo appearance by King as an animal control officer. □

STEPHEN KING'S
SILVER BULLET

DIRECTED BY DANIEL ATTIAS

The Werewolf Welcome Wagon greets Uncle Red (Gary Busey) in Silver Bullet.

SILVER BULLET (1985)

The fourth King film from producer Dino De Laurentiis, the $7 million *Silver Bullet*, is perhaps the first feature film to be developed from a proposal for a novelty calendar (though exploitation fare is often tailored to fit a particular title, or based on sample artwork). King relates that he was approached with the calendar idea by specialty publisher Christopher Zavisa at the 1979 World Fantasy Convention in Providence, RI. The concept was for graphic story artist and illustrator Berni Wrightson (DC Comics' SWAMP THING) to illuminate what would essentially be a twelve-installment Stephen King short story. King had previously worked with Wrightson on the *Creepshow* comic book tie-in and was longtime fan of Wrightson's

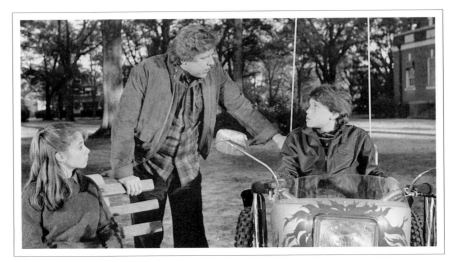

Jane and Marty Coslaw (Megan Follows and Corey Haim) hope to convince Uncle Red that their shaggy wolf story is for real.

SILVER BULLET

A Paramount Pictures release (North Carolina Film Corporation, De Laurentiis Entertainment Group), 10/85. 95 minutes (R). Directed by Daniel Attias. Produced by Martha Schumacher. Screenplay by Stephen King (based on CYCLE OF THE WEREWOLF). Executive Producer: Dino De Laurentiis. Associate Producer: John M. Eckert. Director of Photography: Armando Nannuzzi. Editor: Daniel Lowenthal. Original Music: Jay Chattaway. Production Design: Giorgio Postiglione. Costume Designer: Clifford Capone. Creatures By: Carlo Rimbaldi. Special Make-up Supervisor: Michael McCracken, Sr.

Uncle Red	Gary Busey
Reverend Lowe	Everett McGill
Marty Coslaw	Corey Haim
Jane Coslaw	Megan Fellows
Nan Coslaw	Robin Groves
Bob Coslaw	Leon Russom
Sheriff Joe Haller	Terry O'Quinn

Also: Bill Smitrovitch, Joe Wright, Kent Broadhurst, Heather Simmons, Rebecca Fleming, Lawrence Tierney, James A. Baffico, William Newman, Sam Stoneburner, Lonnie Moore, Rick Pasotto, Cassidy Eckert, Wendy Walker, Michael Lague, Myra Mailloux.

work. The writer responded to this unique narrative concept. He was intrigued by the possibilities in adopting time-honored werewolf lore, with its attendant lunar cycles, to the monthly calendar format. (Later, King would write an introduction for a lavishly illustrated edition of FRANKENSTEIN that had taken Wrightson almost ten years to complete.)

"I suggested the idea of a small town that would have an incursion, some sort of outside supernatural force: a werewolf," King told a reporter. "I liked that because werewolves are full moon creatures and every month there's a full moon."

But the resulting episodes proved too unwieldy for a calendar. Wrightson ended up illustrating a limited edition twelve-chapter novella instead, entitled CYCLE OF THE WEREWOLF. The book was originally published under Zavisa's Land of Enchantment imprint in a variety of hardcover editions, and was later released as a mass market trade paperback by King's paperback publisher, New American Library. King sent an early copy of the work to De Laurentiis, who optioned it and hired him to write the screen adaptation.

The original story is basically a series of bloody vignettes occurring over a year's time in the small town of Tarker's Mill, Maine. About halfway through this series of murders we meet the young Marty Coslaw and his souped-up motorized wheelchair, the Silver Bullet. The open-minded young lad turns detective and discovers that Reverend Lowe, the town minister, has been incorporating his parishioners into the food chain. The kid and the beast have their

Owen Knopler (left) and Lawrence Tierney aren't hunting ducks, they're dispensing private justice.

final confrontation just as December rolls around. Lycanthropy ensues.

The screen version brings Marty and the rest of the Coslow family to the fore. The character of his alcoholic Uncle Al, now named Red, is also considerably beefed up. Instead of spanning an entire year, the film's action occurs during the late spring and fall seasons. Additionally, the werewolf minister is shown in more sympathetic light, which brings him closer to the traditional Universal Pictures brand of werewolf. On-screen, Reverend Lowe is truly troubled by his predatory predilections and has lost the cruel sense of black humor he displayed to telling effect in the book.

With Martha Schumacher (*Cat's Eye*) on board as producer, Daniel Attias was hired to direct. The first-time director had previously worked with both Francis Coppola and Steven Spielberg, and was the assistant director on De Laurentiis's *Firestarter*. Attias worked on the script with King to bring more focus to the relationships between the Coslow family members: Marty's older sister, who resents the attention her brother's handicap affords him; Marty's distancing parents, who seem to resent his condition in the first place; and Uncle Red, another family outcast but the only adult who treats Marty as a person. Through their experiences with the supernatural menace they grow as people (and all that other important

Make my night: Uncle Red, aiming to please, greets the big, bad werewolf in the climax of Silver Bullet.

A furious Reverend Lowe (Everett McGill) overreacts to a temporary dipilatory shortage in Tarker's Mills.

script stuff that film instructors talk about).

Unlike the expensive and cast-heavy *Firestarter*, the De Laurentiis *Silver Bullet*'s $7 million budget was primarily targeted for the screen, not the marquee. All the big names hadn't saved *Firestarter*'s ashes, so now with less to lose it seemed wiser to put more value on the screen. The always reliable Gary Busey (*The Buddy Holly Story*, *Insignificance*, *Lethal Weapon*) assayed the role of Uncle Al, and Everett McGill (*Dune*, *Heartbreak Ridge*) played the beastly minister. (McGill also starred in *Quest for Fire*, but was virtually unrecognized under the Oscar-winning special make-up.) Marty and Jane Coslow were played by Corey Haim (*Lucas*) and Megan Follows.

As he had with the troll in *Cat's Eye*, Carlo Rimbaldi was again charged with devising a fully-articulated puppet head, this time for the werewolf. De Laurentiis wanted something unusual and three different versions were created before a final design was approved. These prototypes were certainly unusual—they were more like were-bears or were-apes than the standard Hollywood models. But the effect was considered a bit too outre and was finally abandoned for what could be called a weredog design.

As with the troll mask in *Cat's Eye*, the non-electronic, cable-ac-

The topic of today's eulogy is "Don't fear the terror that creepeth by night, the face of the beast always becomes known."

tuated werewolf head (using the same principles as bicycle handbrakes) required four people working twelve levers to make it come to life. (It would even be able to speak specific lines of dialogue.) The device was designed to fit over a full bodysuit, resulting in a complicated but effective special effects make-up that was actually rather easy to handle and prepare for filming. Choreographing all the right lever moves for a convincing "performance" required hours of laborious practice, but evoked a more lifelike illusion than similar computer-actuated devices. A second, non-actuated head was also made for action scenes and mid-range shots.

Also on the werewolf trail was special make-up artist Michael McCracken, Jr., another previous De Laurentiis team player. His job was to handle the werewolf transformation scenes, not just the Reverend Lowe's (a combination of air bladders and lap-dissolves), but also in a vivid dream sequence where Lowe's congregation begins changing into wolves. This scene required the services of some forty dancers and gymnasts—all wearing one of three varying versions of complex special make-up (as dictated by their relative closeness to the camera)—making it the largest werewolf gathering ever filmed. For this sequence the werewolf make-up was kept much more human in tone, closer to the classic Wolfman version of the old Universal pictures.

The picture's location shooting was done in Burgaw, NC, deemed a reasonable incarnation of Maine and still convenient to the De Laurentiis studios in Wilmington.

The finished product is by no means a definitive statement on werewolf culture; nor is it a very imaginative horror film. King's script is traditional in plot and characterization, and offers no explanation for Reverend Lowe's condition. Lowe seems just to have somehow contracted a dose of lycanthropy, and his final "back from the dead" throes are by now a tired cliche. Still, *Silver Bullet* is an entertaining and unpretentious picture and despite the R rating for violence it works well as a kid's adventure (especially given the family subplot).

De Laurentiis once again demonstrated his willingness to develop almost anything that Stephen King has a hand in, regardless of the project's other qualities. The commercial response to *Silver Bullet* was much like the film itself, not anything special. The picture did make its money back at the domestic box office, however. □

"That idea started as a calendar, with Berni [Wrightson] doing the illustrations for 12 separate months but with some kind of continuity, as though it were a story.

"I suggested the idea of a small town that would have an incursion, some sort of outside supernatural force: a werewolf. I liked that because werewolves are full moon creatures and every month there's a full moon. I thought here we can have 23 new and interesting murders, sort of like FRIDAY THE THIRTEENTH—except that in itself seemed to be very shaky, like snuff stuff, set 'em up and knock 'em down like dominoes.

"A story did develop out of it, however, but the individual pieces were too long to do a calendar so it's now done as a book with the illustrations and the twelve months."
—Speaking of *Silver Bullet* with Edwin Pouncey

DIRECTED BY STEPHEN KING

The 55 mile-an-hour speed limit goes by the wayside as the happy Toyz truck delivers another load of joy.

MAXIMUM OVERDRIVE (1986)

In 1985 De Laurentiis acquired his own distribution system through the purchase of Embassy Pictures. Coupled with his North Carolina studio facilities, this gave De Laurentiis the status of a full-fledged "mini-major." The De Laurentiis Entertainment Group (DEG) is one of the newer players (albeit with a seasoned coach) on the production/distribution playing field, in a game that had been dominated by the major studios since the Twenties.

(Before the Consent Decrees in the late Forties severed their

"Your bank express card—don't leave home without it!" Stephen King's pre-credits cameo in Maximum Overdrive.

MAXIMUM OVERDRIVE

A De Laurentiis Entertainment Group release, 8/86. 95 minutes (R). Directed by Stephen King. Produced by Martha Schumacher. Original Screenplay by Stephen King. Executive Producers: Mel Pearl & Don Levin. Director of Photography: Armando Nannuzzi. Editor: Clifford Capone. Music: AC/DC. Production Design: Giorgio Postiglone. Costume Designer: Clifford Capone. Make-up Special Effects: Dean Gates. Special Effects Coordinator: Steven Galich.

Bill Robinson	Emilio Estevez
Hendershot	Pat Hingle
Brett	Laura Harrington
Connie	Yeardley Smith
Curt	John Short
Wanda June	Ellen McElduff
Duncan	J.C. Quinn
Camp Loman	Christopher Murney
Deke	Holter Graham

Also: Frankie Faison, Pat Miller, Jack Canon, Barry Bell, John Brasington, J. Don Ferguson, Leon Rippy, Bob Gooden, R. Picket Bugg, Giancarlo Esposito, Martin Tucker, Marla Maples, Ned Austin, Richard Chapman, Jr. Bill Higgens.

theatre chains, only those studios active in production, distribution and exhibition were considered "majors." In the Reagan Era the majors are now re-entering the exhibition field, buying theatres, television stations and cable franchises, thanks to a more lenient Justice Department. Exhibitors are also expanding, building new theatres and renovating existing ones, making it easier for independent products to find screens and an audience, much like it was in the Twenties.)

With his daughter, film producer Raffaella De Laurentiis, overseeing company production, DEG quickly became one of the most active new companies in the industry. Reflecting De Laurentiis's commercial instincts and support of artistic merit, DEG released an eclectic array of pictures in 1986, ranging from questionable pot-boilers such as *Tai-Pan* and *King Kong Lives* to the intelligent and controversial *Crimes of the Heart* and *Blue Velvet.*

As mentioned earlier, British film producer Milton Subotsky was active primarily in the Sixties and Seventies with Amicus Productions. This company, which he co-owned, mostly made horror films, including a string of anthology-format horror releases. Several of these, such as *Torture Garden* and *Asylum*, were written for Amicus by Robert Bloch, the American horror writer. (Bloch has been credited by Stephen King with inventing the modern novel of psychological suspense with such works as PSYCHO and THE SCARF.) King has characterized Subotsky as "the Hubert Humphrey of horror pictures—who thinks that all horror pictures should be somehow uplifting. . . ."

In the late Seventies, Subotsky purchased seven early King short stories from an American production company. Three of these, "The Lawnmower Man," "The Mangler" and "Trucks," were targeted to comprise *The Machines*, which was to be a three-part anthology film. Early on, King was approached by Subotsky about writing and directing adaptations of all or part of the material. King demurred. Referring to the stories, he later told a reporter, ". . . I know that if Subotsky made it, it would actually be worse than if they were never made at all. I don't like to root for my things not to be made, except in certain cases, *but . . .*"

Needless to say, Subotsky proceeded without the writer's input. He commissioned Edward and Valerie Abraham to draft a screenplay using the three King stories. The husband and wife writing team had previously scripted *The Monster Club* in 1980, Subotsky's last

From Right, Pat Hingle, Emilio Estevez, Laura Harrington and Pat Miller admire the view at the Dixie Boy.

produced film. Shortly after that film's release, Subotsky and Max J. Rosenberg, the other half of Amicus Productions, became involved in a lengthy, expensive, and less than amicable legal row.

Burdened with court costs, Subotsky sold off some of his King story rights to the De Laurentiis organization. Two stories were eventually used in the Martha Schumacher-produced *Cat's Eye*. Now, with *The Machines* script in hand, Subotsky tried to find American financial backing, but to no avail. Again, Schumacher (now head of production at De Laurentiis) and Subotsky did some business. Schumacher initially purchased all three "mechanical" stories for development, but, apparently having convinced King to act as screenwriter, ultimately concentrated solely on "Trucks."

Subotsky believes King's claims of never having read the Abrahams' work, but he has made noises about certain conceptual elements contained in the non-"Trucks" segments of his commissioned screenplay finding their way into *Maximum Overdrive*, King's "Trucks"-derived screenplay. Whatever the case, Subotsky received a co-producer's credit at the end of another De Laurentiis/King film (as he had with *Cat's Eye*).

Maximum Overdrive was apparently into preproduction before King decided that, yeah sure, he'd like to direct the picture himself. (Reportedly, his screenplay had over a thousand specified camera angles—most Hollywood scripts have less than 10, if any). Admitting to being tired of being asked why the films of his books had, for the most part, turned out to be so disappointing, King rationalized that with all these people ruining his material, he might as well have a go himself. "I wanted to do it once because I thought I might be able to do a better job than some of the people who have done it," King has stated. He was sure he couldn't do any worse. Of course, with total control comes total responsibility as well.

So King signed up—another first-time director Dino took a flyer on. The writer was to have the rare luxury of learning how to direct by helming his own $10 million picture. Talk about on the job training! The results? Well, it *was* in focus.

The "Trucks" story is a *Twilight Zone* kind of affair, pitting Mankind against suddenly sentient, and pissed off, semi-trucks; sort of a "Night of the Living Big Rigs" deal. For *Maximum Overdrive*, King expanded this concept to include the rest of the mechanized kingdom, from soft drink dispensers to electric knives to lawnmowers to—you get the idea. And, like *The Birds* (and Romero's *Dead* films), the storyline concerns those few plucky survivors; that group of disparate people thrown together in this trying time of fantastical crisis. Yes, mayhem ensues.

Leading "Brat Pack" member Emilio Esetevez (Martin Sheen's oldest son and now a promising writer/director in his own right) was signed to star in the $10 million dollar production. He plays Bill Robinson, a short order cook at the greasy old Dixie Boy Truck Stop. Before the marauding big Macks show up, he's constantly harassed by the sleazeball owner, Hendershot, played by character actor Pat Hingle. Lesser-known lights flesh out the rest of King's cross-section of Freeway Culture.

As with *Silver Bullet*, the bulk of the film's budget was put on the screen, not in stars' pockets. The Dixie Boy's highway oasis was an elaborate, full-scale roadside set near the Wilmington studios (a local newspaper ad had to be placed to let the locals know that it was really a movie prop). The set was then duplicated in exact miniature by modelmaker Emilio Ruiz (*Cat's Eye*). As the Dixie Boy also housed Hendershot's collection of stolen Army munitions, the film's 90 minutes of extensive stunts, pyrotechnical work and gore effects culminated in the spectacular destruction of both life-size and miniature sets. The fiery destruction of the Dixie Boy was achieved by blowing the full-scale set with thermite and gasoline mixture, and similarly torching the finely detailed miniature. Though far different in scale, the footage from these two sets cut together seamlessly.

Only minor alterations were required to turn normal semis into menacing "driverless" trucks of death. Using simple extension devices, drivers dressed in black controlled the vehicles from behind thin black curtains that sealed off the modified sleeping compartments to the rear of the cabs. The "lead" truck was "the green goblin," a toy company vehicle with an obscenely grinning green visage mounted on the front grill. The specially sculpted prop was highlighted by colored spotlights off camera to heighten its menacing anthropomorphic qualities.

One interesting production element most directors don't encounter is having a bilingual set. It isn't a problem when the caterer doesn't have a great command of the language, but in this case the De Laurentiis-supplied cinematographer, Armando Nannuzzi, spoke only Italian, no English. While King has claimed that no major problems arose from this, others have reported that normal "five-minute" conversations could sometimes take up to a half hour to conclude; not the greatest situation when the sunlight and shadows are moving. Not surprisingly, pre-planning with storyboards was *very* important to this production.

A confirmed hard rock aficionado (he owns a radio station in his hometown of Bangor), King contacted one of his favorite bands about the project, the primal, aggressive and very *loud* Australian band, AC/DC. Like many high decibel rockers, the bandmembers were King readers and horror movie fans. They readily agreed to work on King's picture. Taking a line from the film for inspiration, the band wrote the picture's title song, "Who Made Who?," and made available their other recordings for King's use. The writer/director knows his rock 'n' roll. The resulting soundtrack album, compiled from King's selections, is a virtual greatest hits package containing most of AC/DC's strongest material. When King appeared on MTV as a guest VJ (video jock), he played the title song video which features performance footage of the band intercut with shots from the movie.

Initially, *Maximum Overdrive* received an X rating. According to King, the MPAA review board cited twelve points of specific violence that exceeded the limits of an R rating. (In the United States they count a picture's violent or sexual episodes; to the British it's *intent* that counts.) King later claimed that only two minor cuts had to be made to get the much-needed R certification. Though De Laurentiis reportedly promised not to recut the film himself without King's input, it was contractual that the picture not exceed an R rating. (Though directors may claim to have "final cut" in their contracts, this "right" is usually limited by length, budget, editorial and rating prerequisites. Most mall-located cineplex theatres have "no X" clauses in their leases.)

Overdrive's snipped material is mostly close-ups of gory make-up effects by David Gates, a former assistant to Tom Savini (*Creepshow*). These shots included head wounds from a salvo of soda pop cans, skin peeling off a dying man's head to reveal the skull, and a chainsaw decapitation. Another sequence mitigated by cuts concerned a steamroller turning a fleeing youngster into a flapjack kid.

King has gone on record as saying he meant to make a simple "moron movie," nothing more than fast-food entertainment for the drive-in crowd. As *Maximum Overdrive* was a crash course in the directorial process (an undertaking rampant with technical, emotional, artistic and political quandaries), it is just as well for King that his sights weren't aimed higher. It might have been better for De Laurentiis, however. *Maximum Overdrive* opened to near-unanimous critical pans and widespread audience apathy. The picture quickly disappeared from neighborhood screens to reappear in video stores 120 days later.

Later King would state: "I can't imagine wanting to go back and do it again. It's like being one part on tour and two parts day labor and three parts detention hall monitor. I don't think it's the world's most glamorous job."

Even later still King would admit that perhaps he *could* imagine doing it again, but not for a long while. □

STAND BY ME

DIRECTED BY ROB REINER

Chris (River Phoenix), Vern (Jerry O'Connell) and Teddy (Corey Feldman).

STAND BY ME (1986)

Stand By Me is based on "The Body," a novella from DIFFERENT SEASONS, King's four-story collection of original material. (Another of the book's tales, "The Apt Pupil," is now in development). Not a horror story per se, "The Body" is far different from what the public associates with Stephen King's name.

Though highly autobiographical in tone, the story is not a specific episode in King's life. The characters in the story are based on real people, and their feelings and dialogue are indeed as close to King's personal experiences as he could make them; but the impetus came not from King's true life adventures but an incident told to him by his college roommate. "I took the main character and I took a lot of things that I had felt when I was a kid and put them into that

King collaborators: Richard Dreyfuss pounds the word processor on screen while director Rob Reiner controls the action.

STAND BY ME

A Columbia Pictures release, an Act III Production 9/86. 110 minutes (R). Directed by Rob Reiner. Produced by Andrew Scheinman, Bruce A. Evans and Raynold Gideon. Screenplay by Raynold Gideon & Bruce A. Evans (from "The Body" by Stephen King). Director of Photography: Thomas del Ruth. Editor: Robert Leighton. Original Music: Jack Nitzsche. Set Design: Richard MacKenzie.

Gordie Lachance . . . . .Will Wheaton
Chris Chambers. . . . . .River Phoenix
Teddy DuChamp . . . . .Corey Feldman
Vern Tessio. . . . . .Jerry O'Connell
Gordie (adult) . . . . .Richard Dreyfuss
Ace Merrill . . . . .Kiefer Sutherland
Eyeballs Chambers . . . . .Bradley Gregg
Billy Tessio. . . . . .Casey Siemaszko

Also: Jason Oliver, Marshall Bell, Francis Lee McCaine, Bruce Wirby.

character, Gordon McChance," King has stated. "But John Irving also says, never believe a writer when he seems to be offering you autobiography, because we all lie."

Set in King's mythical Castle Rock, Maine environs during the late summer of 1960, *Stand By Me* concerns four twelve-year-old boys, Gordie, Vern, Teddy and Chris, and perhaps the most important two days in their adolescent lives. They have learned that a missing teenager has been struck and killed by a lumber train. Flush with the promise of local renown if they can locate the accident scene, the quartet spends an eventful two days on a trek to see The Body. This potential celebrity status is naturally just a self-deception. It is their natural fascination with Death, with actually *seeing* a real corpse (and of someone close to their own age) that propels the group forward into this "mystery."

The story from King's roommate involved going to look for a dog that had been struck by a train, an element the writer was quick to alter. "I didn't think anybody would be too interested in going to look at the body of a dog," King stated later.

The boys have to hurry—they'd like to get there before the authorities discover the tragedy and cart the dead kid away. Though unaware of it, they are in a corpse-hunting race with a local gang of mangy, proto-hood teenagers. The four boys' journey, the stories, dreams and fears they share lead to a moving climactic confrontation. Maturity ensues.

In Hollywood there are only a few ways for creative people to get into the business, especially if they're not rich and don't have industry relatives. They can attach themselves to a property by optioning a screenplay. Or they can bring some talent to the creative end, such as writing the script. This latter method *can* work. But as screenwriters Raynold Gideon and Bruce Evans discovered with their original script of *Starman*, their original vision and the finished picture, with various rewrites and input from other "creative" elements, are often poles apart.

That is why so many writers vie to become "hyphenates": industry talk for writer-directors, writer-producers (very common in television), producer-directors, and various other combinations. Their desires are motivated by simple self-preservation. Having another "creative element" hat to wear helps to protect their original material from the indelicate hands of the committee process that by necessity makes most films. Or, if directing and producing are their ultimate

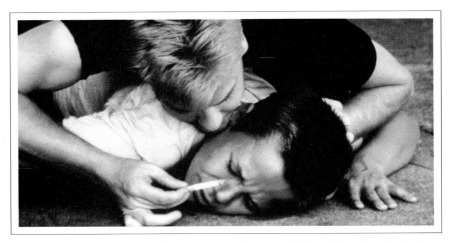

Smoke gets in your eyes: The town lowlife, Ace (Kiefer Sutherland) elicits a painful retraction from Chris.

goal, starting out as a screenwriter can be a solid stepping stone in getting there.

After their *Starman* experiences, Gideon and Evans became writer-producers, and the first project they wanted to tackle was a novella by Stephen King they had read in December of 1983.

Most of these deals work this way: a property (book, original screenplay, life story, etc.) is optioned for a specific length of time, usually a year with the right to renew for another year. A deposit fee is paid against a larger purchase price, securing the producer's option. If the producer is able to arrange for getting the picture made, he then exercises this option by paying the full purchase as previously agreed, usually upon the commencement of the production's principal photography. (Any bonuses or revenue participations would come after the picture's release.) So a property's final purchase price might be a million dollars or more with various participations and bonuses, but it can still be merely optioned for as little as $500 and dinner at a joint on Melrose where a guy in a red coat wants $5.00 to park your car on the street.

According to a reliable industry source, Stephen King's "standard" deal at that time in his career (1983/84) called for full purchase payment up front (in the $100,000 range) and a hefty 10% of the film's gross rentals. (His reported $1 million fee for *Firestarter* was likely a flat price with no gross percentages.) This is a telling testimony to King's marketplace clout, even after the poor performances of *Firestarter*, *Cat's Eye* and *Silver Bullet*. Only a few actors, and even fewer directors, are able to get a "gross participation" deal as part of their fee without having to take an equity position in the picture. A gross participation deal means that rather than sharing in the picture's elusive net profits (net participation), which are calculated after a previously-negotiated definition of "break even" has been reached (often a set figure or simple formula), King gets ten cents of *every* film-rental dollar, starting from the get-go. If King were to write the screenplay as well, this arrangement is probably adjusted with further fees and bonuses.

Gideon and Evans did not have $100,000 in discretionary funds. The only people who do are development companies (usually funded through limited partnerships, or the increasingly popular over-the-counter offerings), the various studios (film distributors), and very successful independent producers. The pair, after some negotiation, hooked up with their friend, director Adrian Lyne, who was then very hot after doing *Flashdance* for Paramount. But given the nature of King's story, it still took Gideon and Evans nearly a year to find a studio willing to fund them. Finally, a deal was made with Embassy Pictures, a young "minimajor" owned by Norman Lear (the creator of *All in the Family* and one of the wealthiest men in America) and partner Jerry Perenchio. "The Body" was purchased by Embassy. Gideon and Evans began writing the screenplay version.

Helping with script rewrites was Andy Scheinman, who gave a copy to director Rob Reiner for his opinion. Reiner, who had never been a King fan, was quite taken with the story of the four boys. He told Scheinman that he'd love to direct the picture if Lyne became unavailable. This came to pass when post-production work ran over on the steamy, sex-obsession melodrama *9½ Weeks* and Lyne informed the producers that he wouldn't be free for a new assignment until 1986.

With Reiner now on the project, his third feature after the satiric *This Is Spinal Tap* rockumentary and the well-received teen-comedy *The Sure Thing*, another series of rewrites took place. These attempted to translate King's interior monologues into a dramatic, theatrical structure. These joint sessions were reported to be quite rocky. Reiner decided that Gordie's character, the burgeoning young

Lard Ass (Andy Lindberg) bulks up for his blueberry surprise in the barf-o-rama story Gordie tells by the fire.

writer, should be used to center the story, providing both a narrative voice and larger perspective for the events to play upon.

The film was modestly budgeted around $8 million (today's industry average is between $14 and $17 million), with a 60 day shooting schedule. Once again, the north Pacific coastline would double for King's Castle Rock, Maine. The film crew hied themselves to Eugene, Oregon, their base for primary principal photography in the smaller, nearby locations. But a far greater problem than scaring up suitable locations was that of finding suitable actors to play the four leads. Almost no adults are featured in the story, so the filmmakers couldn't look to big names for instant box office appeal.

After extensive auditions, videotaping various pairs and quartets of kids to test their on-screen chemistry, River Phoenix (*Explorers, Mosquito Coast*) was cast as Gordie's best friend, Chris. He was quickly followed by Will Weaton as Gordie, Cory Feldman (*Gremlins, Goonies*) as Teddy, and Jerry O'Connell (with no previous credits) as Vern. Keifer Sutherland (Donald's son) portrayed the head teen thug who loves to give the kids grief whenever possible.

Then, on June 15, 1985, after two months of preproduction and just two days before shooting was to begin, Embassy was sold to the Coca-Cola Company, the owner of Columbia Pictures. Embassy's distribution network was then liquidated to Dino De Laurentiis, a story told in previous chapters. But though Norman Lear had left the cinematic playing field (just temporarily as it turned out), he did not leave his buddy Rob Reiner out in the lobby. Lear had known Reiner since the director was 9 years old, and they had worked together on the phenomenally successful *All in the Family* television shows. (Rob Reiner played Mike Stivic, Archie's son-in-law, aka "Meathead.") Breaking the "never use your own money" rule, Lear wrote a personal check for the production and the filming went ahead as planned. Whatta guy!

Production was relatively uneventful and did not go over time or budget. Jerry O'Connell stated that the four young actors totally became their characters for that summer, with their on-screen rowdiness often manifesting itself off screen. (The quartet's motel swimming pool mysteriously drained itself one night.)

The production's most hazardous sequence involved a 150 yard long, 90 foot high wooden train-trestle. In the film, three of the boys are crossing it on foot just as a lumber train comes around the bend. Safety-lines were used for shooting the close-ups and doubles in the long shots. The shot of two of them narrowly escaping the same fate as the subject of their quest (a script device often referred to as "rhyming") was accomplished on a Hollywood soundstage during postproduction. An in-camera matte system devised by the Introvision company was employed to combine the boys leaping from a simple foreground set with a live-action background plate of the deadly train (taken during location photography).

After a rough cut of the film had been assembled, a distribution deal was sought, since Lear's largesse had made a distributor's involvement unnecessary at that point. Just as with the script before it, every major studio in Hollywood passed on the little non-genre film starring four unknown 12-year olds who spend 90 minutes smoking, swearing, and wandering around in the woods looking for a stiff. Though Lear was undaunted, it was Reiner's agent who ultimately conned Columbia's then-chairman, Guy McElwaine, to personally look at the film. Soon, Lear had recouped his investment and

"It should have been me. I'm no good." After the discovery of the body by the river, Chris tries to console Gordie.

then some as Columbia paid for the rights to distribute the picture. But not without changes.

A series of test screenings had convinced the filmmakers to alter the pair of "bookending" sequences where Gordie's character, now a functional, normally adjusted adult (even if he is a writer), learns of the death of his best friend from childhood and begins telling us the story of the last great summer the four friends spent together. The picture concluded by returning briefly to the writer. The film had been tested with, without and with half of the two scenes, but the response indicated that something more was needed. A different actor was used for new bookends and these tested better. Columbia bought the picture in this version. Finally, Richard Dreyfuss was hired to reshoot these sequences and redo the voice-over narration.

Now a carefully plotted marketing plan had to be formulated and enacted. "Small" films like this die commercially all the time due to improper marketing "placement." A non-genre, non-star picture often needs a longer incubation time for strong word-of-mouth to generate. Columbia's campaign for the picture is a textbook example for correctly perceiving the audience for the film and then making that audience aware of the film.

The decision was made to "platform" the film and work on building audience awareness through reviews and articles in the media. Platforming is much like the old "road show" engagements that studios gave their lavishly-produced "A" pictures, a practice that, along with their splashy premieres and reserved-seat tickets, died out some twenty years ago. Today, the practice addresses two vital marketing elements. First, by guaranteeing an engagement for several weeks, the audience has a more reasonable chance of discovering the picture. And secondly, while the per-screen costs are high, at times even unprofitable, platforming, opening regionally, is substantially cheaper than a $7 million full-blown, nationwide opening. If the film catches on, more screens are duly added. If it's a dud the distributor quietly withdraws the film, taking consolation in the fact that greater losses were not incurred.

First off, Columbia knew they did not want the picture mistaken as another Stephen King horror movie. So, not only was King's name "buried" amongst the secondary credits in the ads and poster (Dreyfuss was not mentioned at all), the film was retitled *Stand By Me*, after the classic Ben E. King song that had become the film's major theme. (Instrumental versions of the song are beautifully reorchestrated throughout by composer Jack Nitzsche, and the original is used as well.)

The picture was opened at the tail end of summer, playing just one or two theatres in a few major cities. Critics and audiences responded. As positive reviews and good word-of-mouth built, the film gradually "went wider" to around 700 theatres. This is the exact opposite of the 1500 print "at-a-theatre-near-you"-type openings Stephen King films usually enjoy. And, unlike most of King's recent releases, *Stand By Me* earned over $46 million in domestic box office during the its first 17 weeks of release. It helped give Ben E. King's (no relation to Steve, heh heh) career a nice boost, leading to a spot on Carson (singing "Stand By Me" of course) and a music video of the title song, featuring the singer performing with River Phoenix and Will Wheaton. The film's soundtrack album was soon climbing up the Billboard Hot 100 charts—an even greater oldies package than *Christine*'s.

King himself was reportedly deeply moved by the picture, saying it was perhaps the only one to really capture the human flavor of his writing. He sadly noted that his three friends from that time period in his life were now all dead, unable to see themselves and their impact on his life on the screen. □

STEPHEN KING'S
NIGHTSHIFT COLLECTION

THE WOMAN IN ROOM   The Woman

STEPHEN KING
ON VIDEO

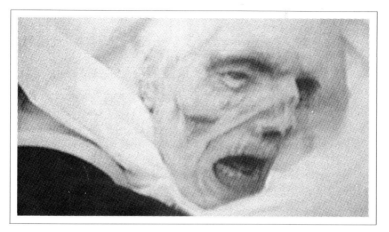

A son's decision to end his mother's struggle with cancer goes horrifically awry.

The Nightshift Collection:

"The Woman in the Room" "The Boogeyman"

One result of the incredible videocassette proliferation is the new market for shorter films via compilation videotape releases. Heretofore unprofitable cinematic orphans such as collections of campy horror film trailers from the Fifties, comedy skits by various artists, and award-winning animated shorts from around the world, these are now being readily adopted by homeprogrammers in their eager search for new and different alternatives to the Top 50 rental films.

In a related development, it is common for film school students to turn to their favorite literary material for inspiration when making their films. In the non-commercial school environment, the normal options and clearances are not usually necessary if a student wants to simply adapt a copyrighted book or story for his or her own academic purposes. In most cases, an uncomplicated "academic option" is sufficient, provided that the student does not exhibit or broadcast the work commercially.

Not surprisingly, the short stories of Stephen King are often chosen for such cinematic interpretation, either with or without King's knowledge. (Several have been shot on video at Hollywood's non-profit American Film Institute alone). So, it didn't take too long for an enterprising video company to put King's name and some previously unseen filmed material based on his stories together into an attractive package. In fact, one video entrepreneur should have taken a little longer, as he neglected to get all the proper licensing and clearances before putting out the two 30-minute films contained in the *Nightshift* collection. Now a legitimate, and higher quality edition is available, and no King completist should miss checking out this tape at least once.

Released in 1985 by the Granite Entertainment Group, *Stephen King's Nightshift Collection* ($79.95 list) presents video versions of King's "The Woman in the Room" and "The Boogeyman," both low-low budget independent shorts ("mini-features" according to the box). Directed by Frank Darabont and Jeff Schiro, respectively, they are based on King stories found in the NIGHT SHIFT collection. (The first version of this compilation tape had a third, non-King horror tale included as well).

"The Woman in the Room" is about a criminal lawyer contemplating euthanasia for his cancer-riddled mother. The idea is put in his head by one of his clients, a Viet vet hitman not in the original story. The film was shot in Hollywood and completed in 1983 shortly after director Frank Darabont and producer Greg Melton had graduated from film school. The pair were able to find some $35,000 in funding, augmented with personal monies, and had independently negotiated for rights to the story with King's then-publisher, Doubleday. The writer had responded positively to Darabont's script and supported him to Doubleday.

The picture stars TV-actor Michael Cornelison as the distraught attorney, Dee Broxton as the suffering mom and Brian Libby (*Silent Rage*) as the contract killer. It was photographed by Juan Ruiz Anchia (*Maria's Lovers*). While the original story was essentially a character piece, it was felt that King fans would expect some kind of a scare. So a short dream sequence with a corpse was created. The prop cadaver came from the Burman Studios in Los Angles, where

Darabont had worked in production capacities on *Hell Night*.

The video was well-received by those who were able to see it, ultimately finding airplay on the local PBS channel. It also made its way onto the semi-final Oscar ballot for best dramatic short in 1983. King wrote Darabont, declaring the work to be one of the best adaptations of his short fiction. The young director recently received a shared story credit on *Nightmare on Elm Street 3*.

Producer/director of "The Boogeyman," Jeff Schiro was still in the graduate film program at NYU when he made his film in 1982. A native of Maine, he arranged for academic rights with King's endorsement (again having to deal with Doubleday). He then had to go back for commercial rights when the videotape package was being put together.

Canadian actor Michael Reid (*Alone in the Dark*) assayed the role of a father accused of murdering his own children in Schiro's Hitchcock-tinged piece. The film copped an award at the NYU film festival but is not as accomplished an effort as Darabont's, the technical quality hampered by the minuscule $20,000 budget.

Stephen King's Night Shift Collection:
"The Woman in the Room"

A Granite Entertainment Group release (85), 1983. 30 minutes. Directed by Frank Darabont. Produced by Gregory Melton. Screenplay by Frank Darabont. Executive Producer: Douglas Venturelli. Associate Producer: Mark Vance. Director of Photography: Juan Ruiz Anchia. Editors: Frank Darabont & Kevin Rock. Art Director: Gregory Melton.

John	Michael Cornelison
Mother	Dee Croxton
Prisoner	Brian Libby
Guard #1	Bob Brunson
Guard #2	George Russell

Stephen King's Night Shift Collection:
"The Boogeyman"

A Granite Entertainment Group release ('85), Tantalus Productions, 1982. 30 minutes. Directed by Jeffrey C. Schiro. Produced by Jeffrey C. Schiro. Screenplay by Jeffrey C. Schiro. Director of Photography: Douglas Meltzer. Editor: Jeffrey C. Schiro. Music: John Cote. Sound design: Jeff Schiro & John Cote. Set Design: Susan Schiro.

Lester Billings	Michael Reid

Dr. Harper...Bert Linder
Sgt. Copeland..Terence Brady
Rita Billings ....Mindy Silverman
Coroner...Jerome Bynder
Denny ....Bobby Perschell
Andy ....Michael Dragosin

Also: Nancy Lindberg, James Holmes, John Macdonald, Dave Burr, Rich West, John Cote, Brooke Trivas.

Tales from the Darkside:

"The Word Processor of the Gods"

Once again George Romero and Richard Rubenstein come on the scene via their Laurel Productions, forging new inroads of television terror. Videocassettes are not the only force whittling away at the dominance of the three major TV networks. The rise of local independent stations and cable, both with original alternative programming, have done much to erode the big three's stranglehold on the television universe. Through independent syndication of original programming, a de facto "fourth network" has come into its own. Syndicators can now offer new material, including popular first-run films and lavish miniseries, which are on par with network fare.

Laurel's mini-budgeted *Tales from the Darkside* has been able gouge out a niche in original-material weekly syndication. After two years the series has earned strong enough ratings to warrant funding for another two years' worth of half-hour episodes. This ensures that Laurel will eventually having enough segments to accommodate syndication of *Darkside* on a daily basis, a practice known as "stripping out" (because daily series are sold in "strips"). The really big money is in daily syndication, a fact aptly demonstrated by the recent record-setting licensing fees paid for strips of the *Cosby Show*.

Tales from the Darkside presents horror and sometimes humorous dark fantasy, often in the vein of the original *Twilight Zone* shows. A second Laurel title, *Moment of Fear*, will be their suspense series, similar in tone to the original Alfred Hitchcock Presents programs.

Tales from the Darkside has been able to purchase material from today's leading horror and fantasy writers, and Romero himself has contributed a few original scripts. So it is not surprising that at least one of Stephen King's short tales would be presented on the show. Originally published in *Playboy*, then in a "year's best" horror anthology and again in King's SKELETON CREW collection, "The Word Processor of the Gods" is much like a vintage Rod Serling tale from the old *Twilight Zone* series. An alienated, beleaguered writer discovers that the "insert" and "delete" keys of the new custom computer (a gift from his whiz-kid nephew) can actually control reality. By the end of the story, the writer has "deleted" his shrewish wife and boorish son, and re-stocked his family by "inserting" in his sister-in-law and his nephew.

At King's recommendation, top horror writer and accomplished scripter, Michael McDowell (TOPLIN, the BLACKWATER series), adapted King's story. Longtime Romero cinematographer Michael Gornick began his directing career with this episode. Bruce Davidson portrayed Richard Hagstrom, writer and master of reality, helping to sell the show's meager production values with his easily recognized persona (*Darkside* episodes rarely use more than one set.) A variety of familiar actors have appeared on the show, from Harry Anderson and Darren McGavin to Phyllis Diller and Eddie Bracken.

Laurel recently began releasing videotapes of their better shows, with each cassette presenting three episodes. The first release in the series features *The Word Processor of the Gods*. A feature film of new stories is also in the works.

Tales from the Darkside:
"Word Processor of the Gods"

A Laurel TV Inc. release 11/85. 19 minutes. Directed by Michael Gornick. Produced by William Teitler. Teleplay by Michael McDowell. Executive Producers: Richard P. Rubinstein, George Romero, Jerry Golod. Executive in Charge of Production: David E. Vogel. Director of Photography: Ernest Dickerson. Editor: Scott Vickrey. Original Music: Tom Pile & Bill Gordon. Art Director: Misha Petrow.

Richard Hagstrom . . . . .Bruce Davison
Lina Hagstrom . . . . .Karen Shallo
Seth Hagstrom. . . . . .Patrick Piccinini
Mr. Nordhoff . . . . .William Cain
Jonathan. . . . . .Jon Mathews
Belinda. . . . . .Miranda Beeson
Narrator. . . . . .Paul Sparer

The Twilight Zone:

"Gramma"

1984 saw a brief explosion of anthology shows appearing on television: Spielberg's *Amazing Stories*, the revived *Alfred Hitchcock Presents*, and a newly revamped version of *The Twilight Zone*. (All of these entries were beaten to the airwaves a year earlier by Laurel's *Tales from the Darkside*.) Absent from the CBS network for twenty years, the new *Twilight Zone* with its hour format, 10 o'clock time-slot, and writer Harlan Ellison as creative consultant, was a greatly anticipated entry into the fantasy sweepstakes. After a faltering season (in which Ellison quit in a dispute over artistic freedom), the show was brought back in an earlier timeslot as a half-hour program, echoing the failure of the original series to make it in a sixty-minute frame. Unfortunately, the show's half-hour was opposite the *Cosby Show*. *The Twilight Zone* quickly disappeared.

The first season aired some truly unusual television. One notable segment was based on Rick McCammon's "Night Crawlers," powerfully directed by William Friedkin (*The Exorcist*). Friedkin was scheduled to do another story as well, Stephen King's "Gramma," a short story which had debuted in 1983 in *Weird Book*, a fan-magazine, and, like "Word Processor," subsequently appeared in a Year's Best anthology and again in SKELETON CREW. The story had caught the attention of series producers Phil DeGuere (*Simon and Simon*) who leaned on CBS to option it.

A long interior-monologue piece, "Gramma" tells the story of a little boy left alone one dark and stormy night to care for his aging grandmother, who seems to the boy a horrible senile old creature dating back to at least the Civil War, or maybe the Crusades. But Gramma is in fact a clever witch (yes, the old woman has "her spells," as the kid overhears) who has big big plans for her rightfully terrified grandson.

It fell to Harlan Ellison to script "Gramma," which was considered unadaptable by many (those interior voices again!). Bradford May, primarily known as a cinematographer, stepped in to helm the segment after Friedkin was forced to bow out due to feature film commitments. The results were both powerful television and true to the tenor of King's work. The kid, George (well played by Barret Oliver), sees his shadow literally sucked under the door of the grandmother's room as he goes to bring her tea. Tremulous voice-overs keep the crucial inner-monologue going, heightened by skewed camera angles and some effective quick-cuts of the grotesque make-up effects for the beastly sorceress.

One effect not used for the show was Ellison's original concept for showing that George had been overpowered by the dying woman: a spider was to have crawled from his mouth while his unknowing mother hugs him. Yes, it was a little too strong for the network's sensibilities. The now standard (since *Rosemary's Baby*) "human being with weird feline eyes" contact lenses trick was employed instead. It's a minor cavil. The show truly was a stylish piece of horror and about as good as television gets. □

The Twilight Zone:
"Gramma"

CBS Television, 12/85. 19 minutes. Directed by Bradford May. Produced by Harvey Frand. Teleplay by Harlan Ellison. Executive Producer Philip De-Gure. Supervising Producer: James Crocker. Director of Photography: Bradford May. Editor: Greg Wong. Original Music: Mickey Hart. Art Director: John Mansbridge. Make-up Artist: Charlene Roberston. Special Effects Coordinator: M. Kam Cooney. Visual Effects Coordinators: Bruno George & David Sosalla. Story Editor: Rockne S. O'Bannon. Creative Consultant: Harlan Ellison. Executive Story Consultant: Alan Brennert.

George . . . . .Barret Oliver
Mother . . . . .Darlanne Fluegel
Gramma . . . . .Frederick Long

CREEPSHOW 2
WHEN THE CURTAIN GOES UP
THE TERROR BEGINS.
GOOD TO
THE LAST GASP.
NEW WORLD PICTURES
PRESENTS A LAUREL PRODUCTION
CREEPSHOW 2 STARRING LOIS CHILES
GEORGE KENNEDY DOROTHY LAMOUR
AND TOM SAVINI AS "THE CREEP" MUSIC COMPOSED BY LES REED
AND RICK WAKEMAN ASSOCIATE PRODUCER MITCHELL GALIN
EXECUTIVE PRODUCER RICHARD P. RUBINSTEIN
SCREENPLAY BY GEORGE A. ROMERO BASED ON STORIES BY STEPHEN KING
PRODUCED BY DAVID BALL DIRECTED BY MICHAEL GORNICK
NEW WORLD PICTURES
R

COMING ATTRACTIONS

From "Sorry, Right Number," an original teleplay by Stephen King
for Tales from the Darkside

The Running Man, Creepshow II, Pet Sematary, The Stand, The Talisman, Graveyard Shift, Return to 'Salem's Lot, Apt Pupil, The Cat From Hell, IT, The Mist, Sorry, Right Number.

The Running Man: Arnold Schwarzenegger (*Terminator*) is pegged to star in this troubled Taft/Barish production, under the auspices of company partner, writer/producer/director Rob Cohen. The near-future science fiction book was originally optioned by ex-wheelchair manufacturer George Linder for $20,000. At that time it was still a "Richard Bachman" title, King's longtime pseudonym for non-horror projects. Linder took it around town and eventually got a deal with the Taft/Barish people, a group affiliated with Tri-Star, a rising mini-major.

The show was originally to star Christopher Reeve (*Superman*) and to be directed by Jim Pan Cosmatos (*Rambo*). But script, budget and personality problems led Cohen to discontinue the project and start over. Three more directors have come and gone and Paul Michael Glaser (*Miami Vice*) is now set to direct the $23.4 million picture about a violent TV-show that pays its contestants big bucks if they can dodge a special hit squad for several hours.

The Stand: King and Romero continue to work on screenplays for this mammoth project about Good and Evil duking it out in the great Northwest after a super-flu has decimated the globe. Will this Laurel Production be two two-hour films, a three-hour picture, an eight-hour miniseries, what? Originally intended as a follow-up to *Creepshow*, the lack of a Romero hit movie since *Dawn of the Dead* (and that only a relative hit) and Laurel's desire to retain total creative control must account for this picture's non-appearance and the current production of *Creepshow II* instead.

Creepshow II: The sequel to *Creepshow* was filmed by Laurel, but not with George Romero or Stephen King repeating their original production roles. Cinematographer Michael Gornick makes his feature film directing debut. Romero scripted three King stories, "The Raft", "Old Chief Wooden Head" and "The Hitchhiker" (originally intended for *Creepshow I*) as well as a connecting sequence that sets up the stories.

Pet Sematary: This is another Laurel project, adapting King's take on "The Monkey's Paw," that classic tale of the gift of resurrection having unforeseen and hideous consequences. Withheld from publication for several years, PET SEMATARY became a huge bestseller for King and is his strongest, most gruesome horror effort since 'SALEM'S LOT. King declared at time of publication that he would not sell PET SEMATARY to the movies but after talks with George Romero, King changed his mind and allowed Laurel to option the book "for a song." King wrote a script and studio backing was sought, but to no avail. Laurel will again be making this one independently, using locations in Maine.

The Cat from Hell: Laurel Entertainment is developing *Tales from the Darkside—The Movie*, a four-segment anthology film. George Romero is scripting Stephen King's short story, "The Cat from Hell" for the production and writer Michael McDowell is handling the three other, non-King, segments.

The Talisman: The epic fantasy-quest novel and bestseller, a weighty collaboration between King and his longtime good buddy, novelist Peter Straub (*Ghost Story*), has been purchased by Steven Spielberg's Amblin' Productions. Epic fantasy pictures have not been very commercial lately, with Ridley Scott's *Legend* and the George Lucas production of *Howard the Duck* being two recent expensive disasters. But it takes just one good picture to turn these trends around. What cinematic incarnation this mammoth tome might ultimately assume is anyone's guess.

Return to 'Salem's Lot: Screenwriter Lawrence D. Cohen's has a version of what might be happening in this small Maine town, some years after most of it burned down. Cohen is also working on a staged musical version of *Carrie*, the film he scripted way back when. Given the success of *Little Shop of Horrors*, a movie-turned-musical-turned-musical movie, Cohen may be on to something.

Apt Pupil: Producer Richard Kobritz ('*Salem's Lot, Christine*) is developing this original novella for the screen. This story, found in King's DIFFERENT SEASONS collection, concerns a high school student's discovery of a Nazi war criminal living in his neighborhood. The project has yet to be announced for production.

IT: King's most recent blockbuster has been optioned for a miniseries on ABC television.

Battleground and *Training Exercise*: Two unproduced early screenplays by King that seems destined to remain unproduced. One based on a short story, the other about Marines.

Graveyard Shift: George Demick is a twenty-two year old filmmaker from Pittsburgh. His filmmaking career was inspired by fellow-resident George Romero's *Night of the Living Dead* and he worked as a production assistant on Romero's *Knightriders* in 1981. In 1984, Demick made an award-winning horror video and, in the best Hollywood tradition of self-made men, got a letter of introduc-

From "Sorry, Right Number," an original teleplay by Stephen King for Tales from the Darkside.

tion from Romero and hunted King down in Wilmington, NC where *Maximum Overdrive* was shooting. Demick successfully inveigled King to grant him the rights to the short story "Graveyard Shift" and the film in now in preproduction.

King's "Graveyard Shift" is a gory shocker about factory workers spending a night of terror being menaced by marauding mutant rats. Screenwriter John Esposito will flesh the tale out to feature length. Demick has also tagged special effects make-up master Tom Savini and composer John Harrison, both Romero collaborators, for work on the production.

The Mist: Dino De Laurentiis wanted to film this novella that appeared in the DARK FORCES original anthology. A script was written, meetings were taken, but Dino never went ahead. A science-gone-too-far tale in the classic B-movie style of the Fifties, "The Mist" details the struggles of a small band of humans trapped in a super-market after a secret government experiment goes awry, releasing hordes of murderous, prehistoric-like creatures into our world. Per-haps De Laurentiis was daunted by the extensive special effects that would be required to adequately bring King's vision to the screen. A version of the script was later performed on radio by Boston's ZBS radio group. □

From "Sorry, Right Number," an original teleplay by Stephen King for Tales from the Darkside.